Make the Right Choice

Reverend Dada J. P. Vaswani (2 August 1918–12 July 2018) is the spiritual head of the non-sectarian and internationally renowned Sadhu Vaswani Mission. He led a life of selfless service and is acclaimed for relentlessly spreading the message of peace, love, brotherhood and reverence all over the world. Under his inspiring leadership the Sadhu Vaswani Mission has built hospitals, schools and colleges and undertaken rehabilitation and relief programmes to uplift the society.

Being a visionary saint Dada J. P. Vaswani's illustrious life helped millions to understand the meaning of life. He has spoken on several global platforms on subjects including vegetarianism, animal rights, forgiveness, women empowerment, new education and many more. He is also widely acclaimed as an author and poet, and has written over 150 self-help and inspirational books, some of which have been translated into seventeen world languages. His timeless wisdom and wit and humour have illumined the lives of many.

Make the Right Choice

J. P. VASWANI

PAN

First published 2019 by Pan
an imprint of Pan Macmillan Publishing India Private Limited,
707, Kailash Building
26 K. G. Marg, New Delhi – 110 001
www.panmacmillan.co.in

Pan Macmillan, 20 New Wharf Road, London N1 9RR
Basingstoke and Oxford
Associated companies throughout the world
www.panmacmillan.com

ISBN 978-93-86215-70-3

3 5 7 9 8 6 4 2

Typeset by Manmohan Kumar
Printed and bound in India by Replika Press Pvt. Ltd.

CONTENTS

PREFACE

You can choose to be what you wish to be!

Your life, future, dreams, and your destiny are in your own safe and capable hands. To shape your life and destiny, all you need to do is make the right choice to bring about the positive transformation you seek.

Yes! You have the power (*shakti*) within you, that can transform your life. You have the ability to uncover the potential in yourself; to rewrite the story of your life; to take charge of your own life; to discover the joy that is your birthright; to live life like a prince or a princess, as you are a child of God, who is the King of kings.

God endowed each one of us with Free Will, and all of us have the freedom to change our destiny at every point in life. In other words, we have the freedom of choice to act; to choose between right and wrong. At every step of life, we can make the effort to improve our condition. Through our actions, we can actually succeed in changing our own *karma* and thus altering our own destiny.

We should not ignore the darker side of this power of choice: even as I write this, and while you read this, thousands of people have chosen to drink and drive, and are involved in fatal road accidents. And without offending the delicate sensibilities of my readers, I must also point out that rape, murder, and assault statistics are so horrifying when we consider how many individuals choose violent crimes every minute, every moment, here on this good earth.

This little book is all about the choices we make, every living moment.

Don't you believe me when I say you are making a choice every moment? Right now, at this very moment, you could have been surfing the internet idly; you might even have chosen to smoke a cigarette or order a pizza, instead, you have chosen to read this book.

You may be familiar with that remarkable young man, Nachiketas, whose story is told in the *Kathopanishad*. Nachiketas' father is performing a *yajna* that will enable him to go to heaven. That is surely the greatest gift a man can ask for in this life, don't you think? As part of the requirements of the *yajna,* gifts have to be given away to *brahmins* and poor folk. When he sees his father giving away old and ailing cows as *daan* (alms) in the *yajna,* Nachiketas protests that he must be true to the spirit of the scriptural injunctions, and insists that his father should give away more worthwhile gifts; indeed, the best he can offer. The father is so incensed by the lad's criticism, that he gives away Nachiketas to Yama, the Lord of Death, as a gift. Undeterred by this, Nachiketas waits without food and water for three whole days and three nights to see Yama. Yama is contrite that he has kept a young *brahmachari* waiting so long, and offers him riches and gifts in compensation.

However, the determined young man was not ready to settle for anything other than enlightenment. 'I have come from the mortal realm,' he tells Yama, 'why then would I choose material gifts and be content with something mortal? I desire only that which is immortal and eternal.'

Yama is pleased with the young man. He has effortlessly rejected worldly gifts and pleasures and chosen truth and wisdom over everything else. In every round of the game called life, Yama explains, man is confronted by two choices: the pleasant, and the righteous. The former leads us to worldly pleasures, the latter leads us Godward. Nachiketas is indeed wise, for he has chosen wisdom over wealth, truth over ephemeral pleasures.

Yama, the wise counsellor, tells Nachiketas that our body is like a chariot drawn by five horses – the five senses. When we are in the driver's seat, we are good and capable charioteers, we keep the horses safely under our control; else, the wild horses will go after what they want. 'The senses,' Yama tells Nachiketas, 'always choose *preya,* the pleasurable path, that leads only to death and ruin.'

Is this not true? When we run after the pleasures of this world, our happiness is only momentary. We think we are drinking life to the dregs, but, in reality, we are just indulging the senses. Excessive indulgence in pleasures can only lead to pain and disillusion, and we end up at death's door, spiritually bankrupt.

Do we have an alternative? 'Yes, indeed,' Yama assures Nachiketas. We can avoid the pleasurable path called *preya* and choose the path of *shreya*. The tough and thorny path that begins in the awareness that we are not the bodies we wear and there is more to us than just the senses and mind; it begins in the awareness that we are immortal souls and our home is in the eternal.

The choice is ours. We have to choose between *preya* and *shreya*. But a question arises: how many of us can really distinguish between *preya* and *shreya?*

'Wait a minute, Dada,' I can hear my young readers protest. 'I don't think I've met these young ladies whom you just mentioned. Who are *preya* and *shreya*?'

Preya and *shreya* are paths we choose to walk this life through. These are choices we make as ways of living. *Preya* offers us instant pleasure and gratification, but its consequences are far-reaching and almost always negative. *Shreya,* on the other hand, involves controlling the senses and their desires, it entails self-discipline and self-control and denying oneself the gratification that the lower impulses crave. But the rewards of such self-denial are almost wholly beneficial and positive in the long run.

There is a young lady I know, who often proclaims, 'If the reward for all this is in heaven, forget it, I'm not interested.' She refers, of course, to the tough choices she has had to make, and rues the fact that she has had to deny herself the soft and easy options. But she is right; she will have to wait for those rewards.

It must be pointed out that sometimes *preya* can also lead to instant ruin. Take the case of a young man driving an expensive, powerful, fast bike that his rich father has just gifted him; choosing *preya* in his case means driving at high speed, pushing the powerful and sophisticated machine to its limit, unmindful of speed limits and other traffic on the road. Choosing *shreya* means keeping to the rules and traffic regulations, resisting the temptation to ride 'fast and furious', as the expression goes.

We are confronted by the necessity of making right choices almost every waking moment of our lives. What do we choose: rash driving or sober speed? anger or forgiveness? indulgence or restraint? falsehood or truth? screaming and shouting or patient explanation? corrupt practices or upright behaviour? And, in the broader context, *dharma* or *adharma?* righteousness or wrongdoing?

On the face of it, the choice is simple and straightforward; but putting it into practice is challenging for some of us. But practice it we must, if we are to avoid the pitfalls, the negative outcomes that *preya* will inevitably lead us to.

You have to choose between two paths: the easy, tempting, alluring worldly path, which will lead you to unhappiness; or the difficult, thorny and painful spiritual path, which will lead you to ultimate bliss. It will lead you to the realm of light.

For this, first, you have to make a choice. You have to make the decision yourself – which path to follow and what goal to achieve.

You will receive in relation to what you choose! For this too is a secret law of nature. The law of 'ask and you shall be given' operates on certain principles. You have to ask, when the mind is integrated and focussed. Normally, we ask for worldly things. We ask when the mind is turbulent. We ask continuously; we are not sure what we really want from the Universe. The Universe is there to give us help, and reciprocate our thoughts and emotions. These secrets of the Universe are not hidden, but are open to everyone.

One thing is for sure, you cannot divide your heart into two. You cannot partition it, and say, 'Okay, on one side, I will have the luxuries of the world, and on the other side, I will have the Almighty, the Illumined One.' Lord Jesus, more than two thousand years ago, had said the same thing, 'You cannot serve two masters at the same time.' Hence, choose your path, choose what or whom you will give your heart to, choose your master, and the choice is most certainly yours.

I pray to the Almighty that you may always make the right choice.

CHAPTER 1

YOU HAVE A CHOICE

A new day dawns . . .

The alarm goes off: you have the choice to spring out of bed or snooze.

You wake up: you have the choice to think of God or think of the world.

You decide to get up from your bed: you have the choice to be grateful for a brand new day or feel oppressed by all the work that awaits you.

Every moment of life offers us a choice. A behavioural scientist tells us that on any given day we make around 600 to 3000 choices consciously or unconsciously. Tea or coffee; sandwich or a hot meal; walk or drive; blue dress or green dress; formals or casuals, the list goes on.

There are many people in this world who do not have the luxury of standing in front of a wardrobe, wondering what they are going to wear that day. But even such people have the choice to pick their attitude to face the day: to complain, whine, or be cheerful and positive.

How often do you choose to smile? It's one of the best choices open to us all.

How often do you choose to be thankful? Ingratitude is also a deliberate choice.

We take immense trouble to choose the clothes we wish to wear, the food we want to eat, the courses we wish to pursue in college, the job we would choose, and the locality to live in. But we must not fall into the habit of making choices based on sheer force of habit or superficial awareness. This only makes us similar to blinkered horses.

The most important choice we must all make is to choose Life, with a capital L; not just living, as a routine existence.

What is it to live truly? It is to make a choice of the values, ideals, and aspirations that truly matter to us. To determine how we live from day to day, what beliefs and core values we cherish, and how best we may fulfil the purpose for which we came upon this earth. If we fail to make this fundamental choice, what difference can there be between us and those beings we regard as 'lesser' than us, namely animals, which live by their primitive instincts and basic senses?

Let me share with you this story that a friend told me. In this fable, God creates a cow first. 'I give you fifty years of life,' He tells the cow. 'You will stay out in the sun and do as the farmer tells you. You will beget calves and yield milk to the farmer.'

The cow is not very happy. 'I don't need fifty years for this kind of life,' the cow tells her Creator. 'Take forty years back. Ten years are enough for me.'

God then creates the monkey. 'You have twenty years to live,' He tells the monkey. 'You will swing from tree to tree, and make people laugh making faces and doing your monkey tricks.'

'Twenty years to make faces and make people laugh? Ten years are more than enough,' says the monkey. 'I give you back the rest.'

God next creates the dog. 'I give you twenty years of life. You will sit all day outside your master's house,' He tells the dog. 'You will wag your tail whenever your master looks at you. You will bark at strangers and guard his property with your life.'

'What?' grimaces the dog. 'Twenty years to sit outside someone's house and bark at strangers? Ten years are good enough for me. Take the rest away.'

Finally God creates man. 'You will eat, sleep, play, and enjoy yourself in the world which I made for you,' He tells man. 'I give you twenty years of life.'

'No, that's not fair!' man objects. 'Twenty years are not enough for a life like that. Give me all the years that the cow, the dog and the monkey gave back to you. That will make my life span seventy years at least.' God agrees.

Therefore, the story concludes, man eats, sleeps and plays and enjoys himself for twenty years of his life. Then he works all day long for the next thirty years and feeds his family. For the next ten years he makes monkey faces and entertains his grandchildren. And finally, he sits outside his house and barks at people who pass by.

What have we done with our precious lives? What are the choices that we have made during our lives?

'The self is not something ready-made, but something in continuous formation, through choice of action,' wrote John Dewey, the American philosopher and educational reformer. Not many of us know that Dewey was hailed as a 'second Confucius' by Chinese students and intellectuals, when he stayed in China for two years between 1919 and 1921, and lectured extensively to enthusiastic audiences. Dewey argued with passionate conviction that the Chinese people should focus on social transformation and educational reform, rather than on a political revolution. But, as history tells us, China, as a nation, made a different choice

'The whole notion of you-have-a-choice is illusory, Dada,' a friend said to me some time ago. 'We don't choose our parents or our relatives; we don't choose when to be born or when to die; we can't get into institutions or courses of our choice due to eligibility constraints; if we accept the notion of marriages being made in heaven, we don't have the freedom to choose our life partners (in any case arranged marriages are the choice of parents and not the couple themselves); and whether one lives in Communist China, affluent America, or in emerging India, you don't get to choose on how much of your earnings you can keep for yourself. So where exactly is this mythical thing called choice that people so eloquently talk of? It seems to me all we have is Hobson's choice.'

This is a fallacious argument! We have created our character and our destiny by choices we have made in the past. But we have the present now, and it is never too late to make the right decisions and choices so that our future is of our own making and liking.

Maharishi Valmiki was a dacoit. But he rose above his destiny to become a great sage and an immortal composer, whose name was attached to Lord Sri Rama.

Siddhartha was born a prince, but he chose the road less travelled; he renounced his wealth and luxury and left his father's kingdom and sought enlightenment. He became the Buddha, hailed as master and guide by millions of people even today.

Every day, every moment, we face crucial choices. Junk food, junk thoughts, junk feelings, or nutritious food, positive thoughts, good feelings; shall I eat a packet of wafers or shall I bite into an apple? Shall I lose my temper or shall I be patient? Shall I be jealous of my neighbour's new car or feel happy for his happiness?

Every choice we make and every action we perform becomes a chain reaction. If only we have the wisdom and foresight to stop and ask ourselves, 'What consequences will my choice bring on me and my loved ones? How will it affect the lives of others around me?'

Don't think this is a far-fetched notion: think of a man who is drinking; think of a youngster who is about to try drugs; think of someone who is planning to cheat or defraud others. Why, you know as well as I do, even crossing the road carelessly or driving your car too fast can have dire consequences! Only, we are not aware of these consequences when we do as we please!

Some of the highest and best attributes of human beings, such as wisdom, insight, discrimination, and detachment are called into action when we make a choice.

Think of a thoughtless tourist who keeps throwing plastic bags, cans, and chocolate wrappers on the beach, near shrines and temples, and on mountain slopes; think of the wise man who picks up the rubbish of others and deposits it all carefully in the trash can. Now, do you realize what I mean?

May I share with you the story of Hobson's choice. Today, we take it to mean 'no choice at all' or just a false illusion of choice. Thomas Hobson was the owner of a livery stable near Cambridge in sixteenth-century England. He had a stable of around forty horses, which were hired by the travellers. But if a traveller saw the extensive stable and paid the money to hire a horse imagining that he could choose any horse that he fancied, well, the poor man was mistaken. Hobson simply would not let his customers choose a horse of their liking. He would point to the one in the first stall and say, 'Take this or leave it. The others are not available now.' Only the worst kept horses were on offer; the best one's were protected for special customers only and prevented from being overused by all and sundry. So you see, Hobson's choice was originally a business strategy.

Do we really have a choice? I think we do. Do we all really have the chance to exercise our choice, assert our free will while we make that choice? The answer again is yes, I think we do.

Let me warn you straight away. There are factors that influence our choice. There is a very strong case to be made out for environmental influences (family, social background, a whole range of social stimuli that influences us); equally powerful is our basic nature or mental / physical makeup (what people call genetics); in short, the whole issue of 'Nature versus Nurture'. But that is not what this book is all about. This is about the choices we make at every moment of our lives, the choices which determine what sort of a person you or I will eventually become.

I believe we always have a choice!

Then there are philosophical arguments made against man's power to choose. One of the key concepts of Taoism is *wu wei*, meaning, 'non-action' or 'not acting'. The concept of *wu wei* is complex and reflected in multiple interpretations of the phrase: it may mean 'not doing anything', 'not forcing', 'not acting' in the theatrical sense, 'creating nothingness', 'acting spontaneously', or even 'flowing with the moment'.

Let me tell you that 'flowing with the moment' or 'going with the flow' is not passive determinism or procrastination. *Wu wei* is a choice that demands right thinking and right action. First and foremost, we need to get in the flow; we need to focus our attention on the present. This means clearing our minds from the clutter of the past, and from the worries and anxieties of the future. It is making the choice to become truly aware and conscious of who we are and what we are doing.

Are these not some of the conscious and difficult choices we must make?

Another Chinese philosopher and thinker, Mencius, narrated this parable about a farmer who returned home late one evening after an exhausting day in his fields. His sons asked him anxiously, 'Papa, what have you been doing?'

'It was tough, but someone had to do it,' the farmer replied. 'I've been in the fields helping the sprouts grow,' he explained. The sons were worried and rushed to the field. All they found was a whole plot of shrivelled baby sprouts, which had been beaten to the ground, practically yanked to death.

Mencius is trying to explain his own concept of *wu wei* in this story. All natural things require gentle cultivation. We need to sow the seeds and water the sprouts, but even more important, we need to let nature take its course. And let the sprouts grow themselves.

Wu wei is not inaction or laziness; it is the antithesis of struggle and strife. When do we struggle? We struggle when we are greatly attached to the outcome or the fruits of our action. When we detach ourselves from undue expectations of praise or blame, reward or punishment, we then act spontaneously, without being anxious about what others think or what we hope to achieve. In short, learning to let go!

I know some brilliant students who study their lessons and do their extra research and reading all year round. They don't make a big issue or show of their hard work. On the other hand, we also have average students who make out that study holidays are a period of intense torture and painful effort when their right to a free life is curbed and curtailed by the demands of the examination system. One sensible mother told me that during the study holidays which precede examinations, her son spent 10 per cent of the time studying and 90 per cent of the time complaining or exchanging messages with his friends. It's a matter of choice.

Choice is not an aggression; choice is not a monstrous assertion of one's will. Choice is, more often than not, taking an informed decision. Sometimes, it is just choosing the right response, the right attitude, to face circumstances. More often than not, the right response to a certain situation may be the good old virtue of patience.

Viktor Frankl, the author of *Man's Search for Meaning* was an eminent psychiatrist and practicing counsellor in Vienna, before he was captured by the Nazis and put in a concentration camp. Amidst the horrors and sufferings of Dachau, he realized that life did have a meaning; and that even if everything including the right to live is taken away from a human being, he would still be left with the 'last of the human freedoms: to choose one's attitude in any given set of circumstances; to choose one's own way.'

Making a decision is one thing; to put it into action is a different matter altogether. Have you heard the riddle about the three frogs on a log? One of them made a decision to jump. How many do you think were left?

The unexpected answer is this: there are still three frogs on a log, because one of them only made a decision, but he did not act upon it.

Decision making is a big step, but it is only half the battle. The essential thing is to make the choice and act upon it.

Here is a list of choices we can make every day:

- Choose God
- Choose Faith: in yourself, humanity, the universe around you
- Choose to be positive
- Choose to be kind
- Choose to be confident
- Choose to face every situation with courage
- Choose to forgive and forget
- Choose to dream
- Choose to believe in the good that all of us are capable of
- Choose to be happy
- Choose to make others happy
- Choose to stay away from negative people
- Choose to laugh, especially at yourself

Exercise

1. *How many times did you lose your temper/patience yesterday?*
2. *How often did you find yourself frustrated/disappointed by situations that confronted you?*
3. *Was there a chance for you to show patience, understanding and good humour to other people?*
4. *Did you make the right choice every time?*

CHAPTER 2

LIVING IN THE HERE AND NOW

Whatever other choices we may confront in our lives there is one crucial choice that we must all make every minute, every second of the day. We must choose to live in the present and not let the shadow of the past or the fear of the future affect our present living moment.

Of course, we are all living in the present, you may retort. We are not in a time machine that can transport us to the past or the future.

True, you are living, breathing now. The present moment is the happening moment, the only reality. But is your focus on the present moment? Are you aware of the sanctity of life, the precious breath you inhale, the sheer joy of being alive at this moment?

Let me remind you in the words of the poet P. B. Shelley. He writes in his beautiful poem, 'To the Skylark':

We look before and after
And pine for what is not;
Our sincerest laughter
With some pain is fraught.

We persistently dwell on what has happened. We agonize over what could have happened. We either become negative about the present or become fearful of the future. We torment ourselves with thoughts of 'would have', 'should have', and 'could have', trying in vain to rewrite our lives in wishful thinking. Surely, we should realize that this is a futile exercise.

So many of us are planning, dreaming, and even strategizing, for the future. We are busy setting up targets to reach and milestones to cross and new territories to conquer. Quite often, we heap huge expectations on ourselves and our lives. We rush to do this, we hasten to achieve that, all without actually enjoying what we are up to.

I am not discouraging you from setting goals or nourishing ambitions. It is certainly good to have goals; but having once chosen your goal, don't lose yourself in idle daydreams and endless speculation. Personal and business goals require that you act on them; and the moment to act is now.

Here is a verse from the *Dhammapada* (a Buddhist scripture traditionally assigned to the Buddha himself, translated by F. Max Muller), which will open your eyes to the truth:

> If a person is awake, aware, mindful, pure, considerate, self-restrained, and lives according to duty, that person's glory will increase. By awakening, by awareness, by restraint and control, the wise may make for oneself an island which no flood can overwhelm.

When we train ourselves to live in the present, we appreciate the joy and the very act of living; we involve ourselves in life and discover its beauty. We learn to focus. We must make every moment count; we must embrace every moment, and cherish living in the present.

Are you awake, aware, mindful, here and now?

Nutritionists will tell you that it is essential to chew your food slowly, relish every morsel and taste each flavour in every spoonful of food you pick up from your plate and put into your mouth. This is essential, they say, both from the point of view of enjoying the food, and for absorbing all the nutrients and learning to eat moderately for your satisfaction. Life is a tasty meal that has been laid before you: shouldn't you savour, enjoy, and live every moment of this great gift?

Mindfulness and living in the present moment allows you to enjoy the richness and the treasure that every second offers you. If you are worried about the past, anxious for the future, irritated by circumstances or just annoyed with someone, you throw away this treasure! Mindfulness gives you greater control, greater awareness of how you interact with people and react to situations. You realize that it is wasteful to lash out in anger, or be consumed by fear. You learn to regulate your behaviour. You become less aggressive, less resentful, and more peaceful.

This is a true story about a young mother who had to quit her job and stay at home to look after her two-year-old son. She missed her carefree outings, happy chatter with colleagues at work, the frequent sandwiches, and endless cups of coffee. Here she was, tied to home, with the little boy stubbornly clinging to her apron strings. She felt she was losing out on every joy that life had to offer. In sheer desperation, she called up a free helpline for young mothers. When the sympathetic counsellor at the other end of the line said to her in a soothing voice, 'How is everything with you?' she just broke down and poured out all her frustration.

'It is worse than being in a prison. I can't take my eyes off him even for a moment; he breaks something or upsets something. He follows me wherever I go, calling, "Mama, Mama!" He won't let me read the paper or watch television, he turns my face towards him to make me look at him and says, "Mama, Mama!" He won't even let me close my eyes for a minute, but keeps nudging me, shaking me and calling out, "Mama, Mama". I am done with him. I can't afford a baby sitter and I think he will drive me crazy.'

For a minute, the counsellor did not speak, and respond to her. 'Please say something,' sobbed the young lady. 'Can't you understand what I'm going through? I've lost everything that I valued the most in my life, freedom, mobility, fun, personal space and time. I'm not sure if my son is worth all this. I'm no longer myself. I'm just "Mama" now, and I hate it!'

The counsellor said softly, 'A few months down the line, when he decides to act grown-up, he will start calling you "Mom". You will no longer be "Mama".'

The young mother gasped. She thought of her 'detached' husband and her insensitive brother talking to their mothers. 'Yes, Mom, no, Mom, no, not today, please Mom, I'm afraid I don't have the time. Just called to wish you Happy Birthday Mom, can't come over today.'

Her eyes fell on the little child clinging to her and looking up anxiously at her, distressed by her tears and her emotional outburst. She dropped the phone and picked up her son with trembling hands and held him close to her. The child wiped away her tears and said, 'Mama, smile please.'

'The best and most beautiful things in the world cannot be seen or even touched; they must be felt with the heart,' said Helen Keller, who could neither hear, nor see the world around her. Let us not allow life to pass us by without feeling and experiencing each moment with our hearts.

On a cold December day, in a Washington D. C. Metro station, a young man wearing a low-slung cap was playing the violin. Literally, hundreds of people passed him by most of them did not even stop to look at him. If they heard his music, they showed no sign of appreciating it. Some threw a dollar bill or a few cents into the cap placed in front of him, though many of them did not really stop to listen him. A few people paused, stood nearby to listen; and left after a while, not giving away any money. Many children who were being held by the hand, wanted to stop and listen to him. But their mothers were in a hurry and children were led away, even as they continued to look at him, dragging their feet as they were hurried along.

The man played for forty-five minutes. As many as 1,097 people, men and women, boys and girls, walked by during this time. Only seven stopped and listened for a short while. Twenty people gave money, but did not pause to listen. The man collected a total of $32.17 during this time. When he finished playing and left, there was silence on the platform, nobody saw him moving away and leaving. No one stopped to appreciate him or smile at him. There was absolutely no recognition at all.

If you are wondering how so many details are available about a not-so-important event which nobody even noticed, let me tell you, the whole episode was observed and recorded on hidden cameras. The whole exercise was an experiment conducted by *Washington Post.* It was part of their ongoing social research on human nature, perception, taste, appreciation, and people's priorities and attitudes.

At that time, no one knew this. The violinist was Joshua Bell, one of the most celebrated musicians in the world. On that cold morning, he had played six of Bach's most intricate and complex pieces specially composed for violin. The instrument he was carrying was no ordinary violin, but a unique, handcrafted piece worth $3.5 million. Just a couple of days earlier, Joshua Bell had played at a concert in Boston, where the show had been sold out and where tickets costed more than $100. People had paid good money just to sit and listen to him play the six Bach pieces on violin.

Washington Post (Weingarten, Gene, 'Pearls Before Breakfast: Can one of the nation's great musicians cut through the fog of a D.C. rush hour? Let's find out') concluded its survey results thus:

- In an everyday environment, at an unforeseen or inappropriate time, people fail to perceive beauty.
- Even when some of them did, they did not stop to appreciate it.
- They could not recognize talent in an unexpected context.

The report concluded (*The Art of Theatre: A Concise Introduction* by William Missouri Downs, Wright, Erik Ramsey):

> If we do not have a moment to stop and listen to one of the best musicians in the world, playing some of the finest music ever written, with one of the most beautiful instruments ever made . . . how many other things are we missing as we rush through life?

May I offer a few practical suggestions on how you can choose the joy of living in the present moment?

1. Let me begin with the Zen Proverb, 'When walking, walk. When eating, eat.' Don't try to talk on the phone when you're driving. Don't sit on the sofa with your dinner plate to watch TV. Do only one thing at a time. When you are talking to someone, give him your full attention. It may be a small matter, but it gives you a sense of the people around you. Give your best to what you are doing. Let all your

energy and attention be focused on the task at hand. When the mind is one-pointed, it is capable of concentration and is free from tension.

2. Take time to live, because life has so much to give. Don't rush through your tasks. Slow down your pace if you are one of those hyperactive, rushed-off-their-feet people. We don't have to be lazy, but we must avoid needless hurry. As the proverb tells us, 'Haste makes Waste'. And a lesser known Spanish saying warns us, 'He who pours water hastily into a bottle spills more than what goes in.'
3. Learn to be kind to yourself. Therefore, learn to do less rather than more. Divide your workday into compartments of one-hour each. Draw a circle to represent a one-hour compartment. Pour into it all the work you can comfortably do in that particular hour. Don't think of the work that remains to be done; it can wait. All your attention must be focussed on the work that you can do during the next one hour. But one thing you must do: you must see that you finish the work you have assigned yourself before you move to the next compartment.
4. Stop agonizing over the past as well as worrying about the future. I tell this to people again and again: you should not make yourself miserable by thinking of the past or future. The past is a cancelled cheque. The future is a promissory note. The present is the only cash in hand. Use it wisely and well. Make the most of it! You will feel more focussed and peaceful. It was Lao-tzu who said:

If you are depressed, you are living in the past.
If you are anxious, you are living in the future.
If you are at peace, you are living in the present.

5. Take time out for yourself. Spend at least five minutes a day in silence. Do nothing. Just focus on your breathing. Notice the world around you. Be at peace within! Pause periodically and observe your own breath.

Exercise

1. *Train your mind to focus only on the present.*
2. *Engage with this moment and be involved with what you are doing. Enjoy every bit of it.*
3. *Are you awake, aware, mindful, here and now?*
4. *Look back on the day that has just passed by: how many happy, wonderful moments can you recall?*
5. *How many anxious, worried moments did you spend in the last 12 hours?*
6. *Did you live all the twenty-four hours of your day?*
7. *Did you make the right choice every moment?*

CHAPTER 3

YOU ARE UNIQUE

During my younger days, there were quite a few people who could not read or write or sign their names. It was a common sight to see people affixing their thumb impressions on cheques and other important documents. As you know, our thumb impressions and fingerprints are unique. One may forge another's signature with passable accuracy, but not another's thumb impression. Each of us has our own unique DNA.

There is no one on earth quite like you, in fact, anywhere even remotely like you, forget about the eight mythical people who are your look-alikes in the world. I am talking about biometrics and personality, not just physical appearance. Today, a skilful makeup artist can make any actor look like Mahatma Gandhi, or Emperor Akbar or Abraham Lincoln. But can we have another Gandhiji or Lincoln with those noble traits and qualities that we so admire? The answer is a resounding, 'no!'

The truth is that each one of us is unique.

A young upcoming singer was compared to a renowned predecessor in the field, and hailed as a second such-and-such star. The young lady politely declined the compliment and said, 'No comparisons please. The lady was indeed great and I admire her just as all of you do. But please allow me to be myself!'

Be yourself! One of the most important choices we must make is to be true to what we really are, and not imitate others for the purpose of popularity or quick success.

One word of caution: when I say 'Be yourself', I do not mean 'Do whatever you want to do.' or 'Live any way you like!' A desperado might think he likes wounding people or looting others or just going around vandalizing property. That is just criminal excess. Our jails are full of people who did whatever they wanted to do and did not bother in the least about all the havoc they raised in the lives of others. That kind of behaviour is irresponsible, perverse and may end up making one a criminal.

To be yourself means being true to your highest self; to have integrity in all that you do; to be authentic and not a pale imitation of another. To quote Mahatma Gandhi, *My Experiments with Truth*, 'Be congruent. Be authentic. Be your true self.'

There may be a lot of people you admire and respect. By all means, take a leaf out of their books; try to cultivate qualities you admire in them, like honesty, hard work, courtesy and reliability. But don't end up being dull replicas of others.

If you choose to be yourself, there is one thing you must do at the very outset: know thyself. Unless you know who you are, how can you be true to your real self? And let me add, don't look at the superficialities of your personality. Remember the teachings of the *Gita*, you are not this body that you wear; you are the immortal soul! Therefore, get to know your highest self. Establish your own spiritual identity. Get acquainted with your core values and beliefs, so that you may live by them. Fix your goals; focus on them; and set your own boundaries – which you must never cross. When you have become well acquainted with yourself and the ideals by which you wish to live, there is every chance that you will live a fulfilling and rewarding life.

It was a wise man who said, 'You were born an original; don't die a copy.'

Let me tell you the story of Markandeya. His parents, Sage Mrikandu and his wife Marudhvati, were ardent devotees of Lord Shiva. Pleased with their devout life and austerities, Lord Shiva gave them His *darshan,* and asked them to name a boon of their choice, which he would willingly grant to them. The couple, being childless, asked the Lord to grant them a son.

Now began a *leela* of the Lord. 'I grant you the boon of a son, even as you desire,' Lord Shiva said to them. 'But you must make a choice: would you like to have a son who is dull and low in wisdom, but would live to be a hundred years old, or would you like to have a distinguished, enlightened, spiritually evolved son, who will die at the age of sixteen?'

Without the least hesitation, the sage and his wife chose the second option: a brilliant son, blessed by the grace of wisdom and whose life would be very short. And thus, was born to them, Markandeya, exemplary and noble in every way. He mastered the *Veda*s and other scriptures at a young age, and grew up to be a great Shiva *bhakta* like his father.

The parents, who had watched him blossoming into a young yogi and *jnani* with great joy, began to dread the approach of his sixteenth birthday. Unaware of the early death which awaited him, Markandeya continued to practice his austerities and study the scriptures.

On the eve of his sixteenth birthday, his distraught mother could contain herself no longer. Weeping uncontrollably, she revealed the truth about his birth as a boon from Lord Shiva, and the destiny that they themselves had chosen for their beloved son. 'It is your sixteenth birthday tomorrow, and you will be taken away from us!' she sobbed.

Markandeya consoled his parents. 'Dear Father and Mother, you chose right for me. Of what use is a long but undistinguished life, devoid of *bhakti* and enlightenment? I thank you and the Lord who has blessed me with piety and devotion. And do not weep, dear Mother, for Lord Shiva is the Lord of death. He will protect me from all harm, and he certainly will not let you come to grief.'

On his sixteenth birthday, Markandeya began to perform a Shiva *pooja* from dawn. Sitting with his eyes closed before a Shiva *lingam*, he chanted the *Maha Mrityunjaya mantra*, and began to focus all his concentration on rudra, his *ishta devata.* As twilight approached, Yama, the Lord of death arrived to take away his life, for which he had been destined by Lord Shiva.

'Come on, boy, your time on this earth is over,' he said to the young *yogi*, deep in meditation. But Markandeya was lost in his devotion; he paid no attention to Yama's presence or his call. Incensed at this, Yama hurled a noose at him, and it accidentally entwined Markandeya along with the Shiva *lingam* that he was worshipping. Out of the bound *lingam*, a furious Lord Shiva emerged, enraged at the insult to his form and the disrespect offered to his devotee. He fought Yama almost to the point of death, stopping short of destroying him only because the *devas* intervened and begged him to have mercy on the god, who was only doing his duty. Shiva relented. Yama was spared, but on the condition that he would never ever approach Markandeya. The young sage was thus conferred the gift of immortality. It is believed that he still lives, a young and pure sixteen-year-old *brahmachari* (bachelor), frequenting shrines and mingling with the devout in disguise.

Symbolically, the legend signifies that Markandeya was a *jivan-mukta*, a blessed soul who had attained liberation through God's grace. He had attained oneness with the Supreme Being and was freed from the cycle of birth and death.

Many of us may not know about the antecedents or indeed the wisdom and insights of Maharishi Markandeya; but many of us wish to be eternally young like him; or rather, look eternally young. His eternal youth is what 'registers' in our consciousness.

There are many rich and popular people around us who are living impoverished lives because they are trying to be what they are not. They wish to cultivate a certain image which they show to the world. So they undergo painful surgeries, allowing their body parts to be tampered with so that they 'look' glamorous.

Succumbing to the pressures of the society and peers to look good and appear young despite advancing years is not being true to oneself; it is losing one's identity for the sake of illusory appearances.

I remember the story of a little parrot who was disappointed over the shape of his beak. He came to his mother and wept, 'Look at the pelican; look at the hawk and the finch; the hornbill and the spoonbill; they have such smart and sleek beaks. Mine is so gross and not cool.'

His mother took the parrot to their old, wise uncle macaw. Uncle listened to his great nephew and agreed that the hornbill and the hawk did indeed have 'cool' beaks. Then he asked the little parrot, 'Do you like eating worms and crustaceans like crabs and lobsters?'

'Ughh!' grimaced the parrot, forgetting his grouse. 'Uncle, what do you take me for? I am not a weirdo.'

'Perhaps you will enjoy eating a few fish?'

'No, I don't think so,' said the parrot, wrinkling his face in disgust.

'Well, that was what the beaks of spoonbills and hornbills were designed for. So they are ruled out. Perhaps you would like switching to a diet of dead rabbits and smaller animals like the hawk? No? How about eating small grains like the finch?'

'Well, once in a while I don't mind small grains, but my absolute favourite are Brazilian nuts.'

'Here, do have some,' said uncle macaw, passing a plateful of Brazilian nuts to his nephew. As the little parrot cracked open the nuts like an expert and ate them with relish, the old Macaw asked him, 'Do you think the hawk, finch, spoonbill, or the pelican can eat these nuts with their beaks?'

'I suppose they can't,' the parrot replied, munching away with his beak full.

'Why are you making yourself unhappy by comparing yourself to others when you really don't want to eat or be like them?' said his uncle, smilingly.

The parrot flew back home, far more contented and at peace.

We are all unique and special. God made us for a certain purpose. Let us try to fulfil that purpose as best as we can instead of comparing ourselves unfavourably with others. Let not our self-concern turn into mere obsession with looks and appearance alone.

You are unique and a child of God. There is no one quite like you in all the world! You must therefore learn to respect and love yourself, because you have to live the life that fulfils the purpose for which God made you.

The Netherlands (which we often refer to as Holland) is so called because much of this country is actually below sea level. Geographically, it is a very low and flat country, with as much as twenty-six per cent of its area and twenty-one per cent of its population located below sea-level, and only about fifty per cent of its land exceeding one metre above sea level. Most of the land below sea level is man-made through land reclamation. Since the late sixteenth century, these areas have been preserved through elaborate drainage systems that include dykes, canals, and pumping stations.

One of the greatest heroes of the Netherlands is a little boy called Hans. He was the son of a lock-keeper, whose task was to open and close the locks on the canals to ensure that the water flowing through them was at the right level.

One day, Hans set out to visit a blind, old man who lived way out of the town, carrying homemade bread and biscuits. By the time he left the old man's cottage, the weather had become inclement, the skies had gone dark and it had begun to drizzle incessantly. Hans walked carefully along the narrow road beside the dyke, shielding himself as best as he could with his cap.

All of a sudden, he heard the unmistakable sound of water trickling, and saw that a crack had developed in the dyke wall just above where he stood. Like all children in his village, Hans knew that if the hole was not plugged immediately, the dyke would spring a major leak, leaving the whole district vulnerable to a flood. Without the least hesitation, he scrambled up the dyke wall and put his finger inside the hole to stop the leaking water.

Soon it was night. The narrow village road was dark and deserted, and there were no passers-by, for it was a cold and wet night. Hans' parents did not come out to look for him, for he often stayed back with his old friend to spend the night.

Hans lay on the dyke wall, shivering in the cold. His finger was almost numb with the pain and chill of the cold water. Early next morning, the parish priest who had spent the night at the bedside of an ailing villager, was returning to his church when he caught sight of the young lad spread-eagled on the dyke.

'Who's this? What are you doing at the dyke?' the priest called out sharply. 'It's me, Hans Brinkel,' the boy replied feebly. 'Please get help! The dyke has sprung a hole and I am stopping the leak.'

In a few minutes, the priest had alerted the people of the neighbourhood and the dyke engineers were called to the location. They set about plugging the leak, but not before their leader had wrapped Hans in a warm blanket and carried the boy to a nearby cottage where he was attended to by the village nurse.

The boy's courage and his natural instinct for safety had saved the entire district from flood.

Psychologists tell us that the basic reason for several 'complexes' and negative feelings is the fact that people are not happy with who they are and what they are. They are not ready to accept themselves as they are; they don't like themselves. This leads to a low self-esteem, insecurity, and negative self-image.

God has made each of us for a distinctive purpose. He has meant some of us to become great artists; some of us were born to become great dreamers and visionaries; some of us were meant for professions like medicine, engineering, architecture or law.

But there are a majority of us who are none of these things. Maybe God meant us to be good human beings; maybe, He wanted us to be the helpers and servers of humanity; maybe, He meant us to be kind, loving sons/daughters/spouses/ parents. Why should we try to alter His divine plan?

We can each contribute our own special and unique efforts to make life more meaningful and beautiful. What matters is we recognize the contributions of others and appreciate them. In the words of Rabindranath Tagore:

> There are numerous strings in your lute
> Let me add my own among them.

All of us, with our individual gifts and skills are like so many strings on God's lute. We will make divine music, when we function together.

Here are a few practical suggestions to build your sense of self-worth and help you to become your own best friend:

1. Realize that you are unique. You have been created with certain traits and gifts that are special to you. Because you are not aware of them, it does not mean you are worthless. Try and find out your special strengths and gifts: your friends/teachers/family will only be too happy to point them out for you.
2. Think of what you enjoy doing: singing, dancing, storytelling, drawing, calligraphy, cooking, or gardening. Recreate the sense of pleasure and enjoyment that you derive from these activities, and add more such activities to your daily routine.
3. Participate in the social activities of your group, your community and your neighbourhood. Do not allow yourself

to become isolated from your neighbours and friends. Connecting with others, participating in such activities, draws you out and gives you the awareness that you are part of a cosmic whole.

4. Give more meaning to your life by finding a worthy cause to which you can devote your energies. It may be an NGO, *satsang*, social service group, or anything you believe in.
5. Learn to be kind to yourself. Do not criticize yourself or call yourself names constantly. Take good care of yourself physically and mentally.
6. Avoid the company of people who put you down constantly. Do not allow others' criticism to affect your sense of self-worth.
7. Make a difference to others, and you will see what a difference it makes in your attitude and personal life. Therefore, go out of your way to help others and make life better for them.
8. Above all, always remember that God loves you and created you to fulfil His special purpose. When you know that He loves you and trusts you, how can you think poorly of yourself?

Exercise

1. *Do you really know yourself well? What are your aspirations and hopes? What are you doing to fulfil them?*
2. *Who are your friends? Do they encourage you to be yourself? Have you considered becoming your own best friend?*

3. *Imitation, Sadhu Vaswani said, is emasculation. Blind imitation is self-destructive. Are you living a life that is a lie, as a pale imitation of others?*
4. *Realize that there is no one quite like you in this world: that you are a unique being created by God for a special purpose.*
5. *Choose to be yourself!*

CHAPTER 4

BE YOUR OWN BEST FRIEND

I am sure you have many friends, some very dear, some very close and some for fun times. I urge you to be friends with yourself. Choose to become your own best friend.

I often tell my friends about the inspiring example of best-selling author Louise Hay. Nearly forty years ago, she wrote a book called *You Can Heal Your Life*. She made a conscious decision not to give the book to any publisher, but to print and publish it herself. The ideas she espoused in the book, she felt, were not in keeping with the general mood or thinking of the 1980s, an age which encouraged success through aggression and strategy. Instead, she decided to start her own publishing venture so that she could share her new and fresh ideas with the world, without looking outside for commercial support. Thus was born Hay House, one of the leading publishers of self-help books in the world. In 1984, when it was first published, the book climbed to the top of *New York Times* bestseller list. Nearly three decades later, in 2009, when Ms. Hay decided to make a film with the same title, the book got back to the top of the same list, and, as Louise Hay remarked with a smile, she became a film star at the age of eighty.

You Can Heal Your Life tells us to value, love, be kind, and understand ourselves, and thus become creators of our own destiny. In other words, the message of the book can be summed up in the context of our own chapter title as: Be Your Own Best Friend!

1. You can become your own best friend in the measure you develop patience, kindness, and gentleness towards yourself and others.
2. As far as you can, stop criticizing yourself and causing pain and distress to yourself.
3. If you wish to change yourself, avoid negative means and try positive methods of encouragement and approval.
4. At least occasionally, allow kind and loving thoughts about yourself to fill your mind.
5. Take good care of your body, which is a temple of god. Give yourself proper nourishment and exercise.
6. Seek the help and support of family and friends when you need them. Be a good source of moral support to yourself.

There is a Zen story about a pair of acrobats. The teacher was a poor widower and his student was a young girl called Meda.

The two of them performed every day on the streets in order to earn enough to eat. The teacher would balance a tall bamboo pole on his head; the little girl would climb the pole carefully and slowly reach the top. Once she got to the top, she stayed there, balancing herself on the pole while the teacher walked around, collecting money from the people. Both of them had to stay completely focussed and maintain their balance in order to prevent any untoward injury or accident.

One day, the teacher said to his pupil, 'Look Meda, I've been thinking about this; from now on, I will watch you and you watch me, so that we can help each other maintain concentration and balance and prevent an accident. Then we'll surely earn a little more.'

But the little girl was wise, she answered, 'Dear master, I think it would be better for each of us to watch our own balance. If we looked after ourselves, we are looking after the other. I am sure that in this way we will avoid any accidents and earn enough to eat.'

Take care of yourself so that you may also take care of others. Those of you who are frequent flyers in airplanes will know that, as part of the safety instructions, the stewardess always advices you to put on your own oxygen mask before you help others. This is not selfishness or neglect of others. This is pragmatism.

Once, a patient who had come to the famous psychiatrist Carl Jung, said to him, 'Dr Jung, I feed the hungry, forgive an offender, and love my enemy, and I know these are great virtues. But what if I should discover that the poorest of beggars and most impudent of offenders are all within me, and that I stand in need of all the alms of my own kindness; that I myself am my own worst enemy who must be loved; what then?'

The answer he received was simple: 'Well then, you must acknowledge yourself in the same way as all others: worthy of your love, compassion, and understanding.'

We all know what Jesus told us, 'Thou shalt love thy neighbour as thyself.' If you have nothing but low self-esteem and a sense of shame and worthlessness about yourself, how can you really love your neighbour the way God wants you to?

Consider the story of Satyakama. Born as the illegitimate son of Jabala, a woman who was a servant maid, Satyakama aspired to attain knowledge of Brahman, and decided to seek discipleship at the feet of Sage Gautama, one of the most renowned Vedic masters of those times. When he asked his mother about his lineage and his *gotra*, his mother was at first distressed. But she took courage and decided to embrace the truth at all costs. She told Satyakama that his father was not known, even to her, because of her position as a slave who served many masters. She adviced him to introduce himself to Sage Gautama as 'Satyakama, son of Jabala.' The great guru was so pleased with this truthful admission, that he accepted the young boy as his disciple. Eventually, Satyakama attained enlightenment.

Thomas Alva Edison was thrown out from school as the teacher considered him to be a 'difficult' child. But the truth was that he was a hyperactive and highly intelligent boy. His mother took him out of an uncongenial school environment and began teaching him at home. Learning in a non-formal environment, he developed a voracious appetite for reading and developed a process of self-learning that shaped him into the prodigious inventor and genius who was acclaimed in the world. Following his own heart, he set out to sell newspapers to the passengers of the new Grand Trunk railroad, and soon began publishing his own newspaper, *Grand Trunk Herald*. Undeterred by criticism or hardships, Edison, who also became hard of hearing due to a childhood attack of scarlet fever, rose from humble beginnings to become an inventor of major technology.

Edison did indeed face setbacks and disappointments. When a friend remarked that several thousand experiments of his had been failures, Edison replied, 'Failures? Not at all. We've learned several thousand things that won't work.'

Abraham Lincoln was elected twice to the Presidency of the United States of America, and was revered by millions. He led his country through a terrible civil war and made the nation strong after a political and constitutional crisis. He was responsible for abolishing slavery. History records more grief and mourning upon his death than for any other American president. And yet, in his lifetime, he was called an idiot, a gorilla, and a barbarian.

When Abraham Lincoln was a young boy, he husked corn for three days so that he could earn a little money, to pay for a second hand copy of *The Life of Washington*. He read the book avidly, and said to a woman he knew, Mrs Crawford by name:

'I don't always intend to do this you know – delve, grub, husk corn, split rails and the like.'

'What do you want to be then?' asked Mrs Crawford. 'I shall be the President,' announced Abraham Lincoln. 'I shall study and get ready and the chance will come.'

The chance came and Abraham was ready to take on the most powerful position in the land: he was his own best friend. He had made up his mind to be a winner.

It has been said that winners make goals, while losers make excuses.

Being your own best friend is not narcissism, or obsessive self-love. Remember, a true friend – a good friend – is one who knows your failings and weaknesses and helps you overcome them. A true friend does not hesitate to warn you when you overstep your bounds. He is never afraid to offer you sound criticism when you go wrong. So choose to be your own best friend.

The truth is that many of us just don't know what it is to be a good friend. Sharing jokes, WhatsApp forwards, having a few restaurant meals together, or going shopping in each other's company is not what friendship is all about. True friendship is about kindness and understanding, mutual affection, support, and genuine caring. Quite a few of us can offer it to others. But when it comes to ourselves, we labour under the impression we need 'others' or at least 'another' to be the recipient of these virtues.

Here are a few things we often say to people whom we really love. Have you ever uttered these expressions to yourself when you are feeling low, down and out?

- 'Now sit down and tell me everything. What's bothering you?'
- 'I can't bear to see you like this, unhappy and miserable. Tell me what's troubling you. I am sure I can do something to make you feel better.'
- 'You know I am always there for you. Count on me. I'll offer you all the support you need.'
- 'Just tell me what's the best thing I can do to help you feel better right now.'

Have you ever said these things to yourself with understanding and loving kindness? If you haven't, you've not been good to yourself.

Becoming your best friend is not limited to a feel-good, self-talk. You need to take charge of your own life and act to make yourself feel better.

If you choose to be your own best friend, there are certain things you must do:

1. Shake off bad habits that lead to self-neglect. This might be something as common as overeating, smoking, or something far more complex, like not being able to say no to others' excessive demands.
2. Praise yourself, pat yourself on the back when you have accomplished something worthwhile.
3. Learn not to push yourself too hard, or punish yourself when things go wrong. Remember, none of us are perfect. So why expect the impossible from yourself?

4. Become more aware of your own needs and aspirations. Devote time and effort to doing what gives you the greatest satisfaction.
5. Learn to love and respect yourself. If you can't love yourself, how can you love others?
6. Take care of your physical and spiritual well-being. Pay attention to your health and fitness. Spend some time every day in solitude and silence.
7. Never ever forget: You don't have to be perfect; you don't have to know everything; you don't have to win all the time.

Exercise

1. *What is your opinion of yourself?*
2. *How do you react when you feel hurt by other people's comments or criticism?*
3. *Have you always been kind to yourself?*
4. *When was the last time you felt good about yourself?*
5. *Have you chosen to be your own best friend?*

CHAPTER 5

IT'S ALL IN YOUR HANDS

Swami Vivekananda proclaimed to us, 'You are the creator of your own destiny.'

Best-selling author and acclaimed motivational speaker, Brian Tracy, builds on this well-known saying. He goes on to add: 'You are the architect of your own destiny; you are the master of your own fate; you are behind the steering wheel of your life. There are no limitations to what you can do, have, or be, except the limitations you place on yourself by your own thinking.'

Many people are either misinformed or have chosen to misinterpret the law of karma. Karma is not fatalism. Karma does not cancel your freedom of choice or free will to act as you wish. You create your destiny by your own thoughts and actions. Therefore, make the right choice in all that you say and think and do: every moment of your life, you are creating your own destiny. Ralph Waldo Emerson wrote: 'The only person you are destined to become is the person you decide to be.'

Choose your attitude, change your thoughts, and you can change your destiny!

Every thought is an energy unit; every thought has an echo. Every thought that goes out comes back to you; hence, be careful of the thoughts you cultivate in your mind. Sow the seeds of good thoughts, and you will have a beautiful life and a beautiful mind.

Thoughts are the basis of the life you choose to live. Thoughts are the building blocks of your character, because you become what you think. You write the script of your life story. You can build a beautiful future by harbouring good and pure thoughts, and transforming negative thoughts into good thoughts.

Many come and say to me that they are losers; that they cannot achieve success in life. They blame their destiny; they say they are unlucky. But the truth is they have made themselves unlucky, by reinforcing negative thoughts.

The universe works like an echo: whatever thoughts you think, will rebound to you. Therefore, be careful of the thoughts you think. Free yourself from the bondage of crippling, negative thoughts, before you seek external freedom. Our thoughts are all-powerful. How many of us can really control them?

The future of your life is in your hands.

Every thought that arises in your mind repeats itself, and forms a pattern. The pattern conditions us and compels us to act on it. Thoughts become our habits. Habits then dictate our lifestyles. Hence, we should take care of our thoughts. We make our own destiny, by deliberately creating positive thoughts. Make them into positive habits; create positive vibrations for the future.

A man may cheat his business partner or a weak opponent; he may commit a sin in the darkness of the night and think that no one has seen him or watched him. But he has sown the evil seed in his life for which he will receive the equally evil fruit. And without doubt, that person will have to eat his own evil fruit. He cannot pass on the results of his 'karma' to someone else. He himself has to pay for his actions. That is why we are advised to be alert and attentive; to be aware of the activity of the mind. Do not cheat anyone; do not snatch someone else's honour or credit. Do not criticize or condemn anyone. Please remember: the universe is open; your own thoughts will bring you justice and accordingly, you will receive the fruits of your actions!

Arnold Schwarzenegger, the popular film star who went on to become the Republican Governor of California, was born in a lower-middle-class German–Austrian family. His father ill-treated him and abused him, as Arnold's elder brother was his favourite. But Arnold had set a goal for himself by the age of ten: he would become a bodybuilder, win the Mr Universe contest in Europe and then enter the American Olympia contest and move to the United States. He trained rigorously in the local gym, even breaking in on Sundays to keep up with his training. He joined the army, just to capitalize on their stringent physical fitness regime, and was put in a military jail for a week when he went out to participate in a local wrestling match without leave.

In 1967, Schwarzenegger won the Mr Universe title for the first time, becoming the youngest ever Mr Universe at the age of twenty. He went on to win the title three times in a row. He moved to the United States in September 1968 at the age of twenty-one, speaking very little English. Later, he enrolled for a distance learning course in order to improve his command over the English language.

In 1970, when he was just twenty-three, he captured his first Mr Olympia title in New York, and went on to win the title a total of seven times. The famous *Los Angeles Weekly* was to say of him in 2002 that Schwarzenegger was the most famous immigrant in America, who 'overcame a thick Austrian accent and transcended the unlikely background of bodybuilding to become one of the biggest movie stars in the world in the 1990s.'

Arnold Schwarzenegger certainly left no stone unturned to write the story of his own life the way he wanted it to be. He did not blame circumstances; he did not blame his parents or his background. He made his choice of goal and followed his dream resolutely.

Life today is such that we have to think and act decisively, we have to consider options before we commit to a certain course; we have to make the right choice at every round of life. The days of thoughtless living are ruled out for sensitive, sensible human beings who wish to live a purposeful, meaningful life, which helps them evolve and does not harm other beings or the planet.

DDT, household cockroach and mosquito sprays, plastic bags, additives in packaged food, hydrogenized fats, so-called soft drinks, genetically modified crops, even that spoonful of sugar, everything has come under the needle of suspicion these days. People have also woken up to the choices before them. They read the contents of packages; they investigate the pros and cons of every product they buy or use; they ensure that they don't harm themselves unwittingly. This is indeed a good thing, for we are becoming conscious of the right choice we must make.

The same care and concern extends to other areas of our lives. *Mohalla* committees invite candidates from political parties to address citizens on local issues and answer their questions. They choose to vote for the candidate who will help to solve their problems. Parent–Teacher Associations advise and support school authorities on crucial decisions to be taken. Activists and watchdog bodies monitor advertisements and TV programmes and protest when offensive material is broadcast.

But I wish to draw your attention to the most important choice before us: how should we build our life?

Before we proceed further, let each one of us ask ourselves: am I in charge of my own life? Am I getting the best out of my life? Do I respond in a considered manner or just react hastily to people and events? Who am I most eager to please: myself, my loved ones, my guru, my superiors, or my paymasters? Have I got serious complaints about the way my life is going? If yes, whom am I blaming for this: my subordinates, my family, my circumstances or God? Do I retire to bed peaceful, contented, and happy with my day's work, or do I fall asleep discontented, unhappy for no reason, and just ready to escape from the day's cares? Do I feel secure, contented and at peace with life, or am I beset with anxiety about the future.

Friends, your own answers should reveal to you whether you have taken charge of your life, or if you feel disempowered; unsure about who is running your life.

There was a shy and reserved young man who fell in love with the daughter of a bookstore owner. He would visit the bookstore whenever he had the chance and buy a book or two. The owner would pass on the books to his daughter who would wrap them up neatly and hand it over to the young man with a smile. He would take the books home but hardly ever did he bother to open the parcel or even attempt to read the books. He would lie down and dream of the lovely smile the girl flashed at him. 'She would never ever love someone like me,' he would think wistfully. 'If only I could talk to her, tell her what I feel about her, but how?'

This went on and on, for days together. Then one day, when he went to the bookstore, he could not see the girl. He returned to the shop again and yet again. But she was nowhere to be seen. Overcoming his diffidence, he asked the father where the girl was. 'Oh, she got married last month and has left the town,' he was told.

Devastated, he returned home and looked at the pile of books, all covered and still in their packages, lying in a corner of the room. He had not opened a single one of them. Now, on an impulse, he opened a packet and took the book out. On the first page was written a phone number and underneath it, in a clear and beautiful hand writing was a message: *Please call me. I would like to talk to you. Nita.*

With trembling hands, he tore away the packaging that had been done by the girl he loved so passionately, and looked at each one of the books: every one of them had the same message inscribed on the first page: *Please call me. I would like to talk to you. Nita.*

He had the chance to make his dreams come true, to marry the girl he loved. But he had failed to act.

Do you think fate or destiny could be blamed for his own folly and thoughtlessness?

Some days ago, we heard of widespread power disruptions in New Delhi. I was told that people took to the streets to protest against constant power cuts; students complained they could not study for their exams at night; elderly people complained that the Delhi summer made their life unbearable without air coolers and fans; water supply was lost; normal life was badly affected.

Let us remember, we are talking about electricity supply; a little disruption in power supply causes so much chaos. What then is our condition when we feel we have lost the power to run our own lives?

In this connection, I would like to share with you the Sindhi experience, I may even refer to it as the Sindhi saga, of freedom. As many of you know, the Sindhi community is, technically speaking, a stateless community in free India; this is because the land of our birth, Sindhudesh, went wholly into the Pakistani territory after the partition of India. Again, as all of you must know, many of my people came into freedom and independence when they walked into independent India, practically penniless, with virtually no possessions except the clothes they carried on their backs.

Today, the (Hindu) Sindhi diaspora is a unique example of a community that was driven away from its native land, became refugees in their own country, and rose like the phoenix from the smouldering ashes of partition, to become one of the most successful and philanthropic people in the world. How was this possible? Let me tell you in the words of Gurudev Sadhu Vaswani:

> 'I believe there is a rich treasure in the tradition, folklore and literature of Sind . . . In the Sindhi soul, there is an immensity, an elemental strength, an aspiration to the Infinite, such as is suggested by the vast deserts of Sindudesha . . . Her poets and mystics, her *fakirs* and *dervishes*, her singers and contemplatives, achieved interior freedom . . . In the simplicity and humanity of her poets and mystics is the seed of a spiritual culture . . .'

Spiritualism, mysticism, immensity of vision and aspiration to true freedom, the Master has indeed captured the essence of Sindhi literature in a few memorable words!

He would often tell his Sindhi friends that though they had left their lands, their property, their homes and wealth, they had brought with them a far more valuable treasure: the treasure of their culture and traditions and their spirit of freedom.

During the troubled days following the traumatic partition of India, Gurudev Sadhu Vaswani urged the refugees from Sind to be strong within. He exhorted them to be self-sufficient and refrain from begging for government help. Again and again, he repeated those magic words which became a *mantra* of positive thinking for all of us: 'Within you lies a hidden *shakti*; awaken that *shakti* and all will be well with you.' I remember, too, his unforgettable call to the shattered community, 'Believe and achieve.'

To believe in ourselves, to believe that we are the architects of our own destiny is true inner freedom!

Exercise

1. *Are you aware of the thoughts that go through your mind constantly?*
2. *Have you paused to reflect whether you think positive or negative thoughts?*
3. *Do you think and make a considered choice before you take a decision?*
4. *How do you wish to build your life?*
5. *Who do you think is responsible for your life?*
6. *Choose to create your own destiny!*

CHAPTER 6

CHOOSE YOUR LIFESTYLE

Once upon a time, there was a little girl who was idling in the garden with her elder sister. The little girl was bored. Her sister was reading a book (without pictures, without any conversation) and had no time to laugh or play. The little girl saw a rabbit scurrying past and disappearing into a rabbit hole. On an impulse, the little girl followed the rabbit and squeezed herself into the hole with great difficulty, but found herself falling down, into a large hall with many doors. She found a small key on a table near her, and tried the key on several doors before she found the door into which the key would fit. But the door was too small for her to go through. Just then she saw a table with a bottle labelled 'Drink me' and she promptly opened the bottle and drank the contents. This made her shrink to such a small size that she could no longer reach the key. Down on the ground she found a small table on which was a plate laden with cakes labelled 'Eat me'. She ate a cake and began to grow and grow to such a large size that her head hit the ceiling.

Most of you would have recognized the beginning of the famous children's classic, *Alice's Adventures in Wonderland* which catalogues the magical experiences that open up for Alice as she makes one choice after another. Alice does not like being bored; and she chooses a life of adventure.

We can't all be like Alice and go chasing after mysterious rabbits down the hole in a garden. But we can and must make choices that will help us live happy, healthy, and harmonious lives!

I tell my friends again and again that the gift of human life is the greatest blessing God has conferred upon us. The dawn of each new day endorses this gift in our favour. I often say that a new day is God's vote of confidence in us; it is his indication to us that he still trusts us to fulfil the purpose for which He has sent us to this earth.

As each new day dawns, we face a choice: we can choose to be happy, healthy, helpful and positive that day. Or we can choose to be dull, depressed, miserable, selfish and negative. The moment we wake up, we begin to make choices.

At every step, in every round of life, we are given choices. There are choices to be made, as God has given us the freedom to choose what we like, in the form of what has been called free will.

We *can* choose what we like! If we make the right choices, we will grow in health, happiness and vitality. If we make the wrong choices, we will suffer from diseases, loss of energy, loss of creativity and loss of enthusiasm.

What will you choose?

'Each of us makes his own weather, determines the colour of the skies in the emotional universe which he inhabits,' said Bishop Fulton Sheen. Choose hope over despair; choose the positive over the negative. Bishop Sheen's life was in itself a wonderful example of the choices a man can make to live a worthwhile and purposeful life. As a young priest, his powerful communicative abilities were noted by the church. Even as he continued to be a professor of philosophy and theology at the Catholic University, he was asked to host the radio talk show, *The Catholic Hour.* The truth was that he was only asked to substitute as a host for the talk show for a couple of weeks in 1930; but he proved to be so popular that he continued to host the award-winning show for the next twenty years. In 1951, he began to host the popular television show, *Life is Worth Living* on WNBC. This show too, was a runaway success, attracting as many as 30,000 viewers every night. It was and still remains the most widely-viewed religious series in the history of television. He was one of the most highly educated scholars of his day; yet, his approach and his way of speaking appealed to the common people and his enthusiastic audience averred that he would always 'tell it like it is'. He spoke spontaneously, without notes or papers, and spoke from the heart. Bishop Sheen actually won an Emmy Award for Most Outstanding Television Personality; was featured on the cover of *Time* magazine; and became one of the most influential Catholics of the twentieth century.

When he was selected to receive the popular Emmy Award, he remarked modestly, 'Actually, I chose to accept this award only in honour of my great writers, Matthew, Mark, Luke and John.'

All this while, he continued to teach at the Catholic University, often taking as long as six hours to prepare for a two-hour lecture. He was invited to talk to prison inmates, and when he realized the impact his message had on them, he made it a special mission of his life to visit prisons and address the prisoners. He never ever refused an invitation to talk to people; he felt it was his duty to carry the message of God to people everywhere.

Bishop Sheen never complained, hardly took time off as we do and never ever seemed to grow weary of a workload, which would stagger most people. He once told an interviewer that the source of his strength and never-say-die spirit came from a choice, a decision he made on the day of his ordination in 1919, which was to spend one hour every day in meditation. He maintained that practice every day for the rest of his life. In his autobiography *Treasure in Clay,* he says that the daily hour was a great source of growth and joy in his life, describing the hour of meditation as grounding and transformative. It often meant getting up one hour earlier on a busy working day; it sometimes meant giving up a few social engagements; at times it was indeed hard. But he never ever gave up on his chosen habit.

William James once said, 'Most people live, whether physically, intellectually or morally, in a very restricted circle of their potential being. They make very small use of their possible consciousness, and of their soul's resources in general.' Bishop Fulton Sheen was a priest, preacher, professor, journalist, a great fundraiser for the Church, a popular columnist and author and a media personality. He never held himself back. He was all that he could be.

If you make the right choice, the gift of a long, happy, healthy, meaningful, rewarding life is yours to enjoy.

Choose God's Love

Choose to accept God's love for you. He wants you to live life to the fullest and not merely exist. Accept His infinite love, and you will find that power and vitality and positive vibrations flow into you.

Begin the day with God. And a good way to begin the day is simply to affirm several times, 'I love you, God. I love you, God. I love you, God.'

It would help a great deal if you could identify at least one spiritual practice for yourself and do it regularly. This might be something as simple as fifteen minutes of silence; a personal-quiet-time of half-an-hour; or a short period of meditation or reading from the scriptures or your favourite inspirational author. Do what it takes to get closer to God; make Him real in your life.

It was an inspired poet who said, 'We receive but what we give.' When we offer our love to God, we receive His infinite love for us. When we offer ourselves and our life to Him, He makes our life blessed and beautiful.

Choose Good Health

Your well-being is not something you take for granted. It is a choice you make! M. Scott Peck calls good physical and mental well-being a journey, a process, an evolution, rather than a destination. The title of his book, *The Road Less Travelled*, is actually taken from a poem by Robert Frost:

Two roads diverged in a wood, and I –
I took the one less traveled by,
And that has made all the difference.

Health is a journey which begins and continues successfully when we travel on the right road, and choose those aspects that will ensure our well-being and enhance our vitality.

My prescription for good health is to entrust your health to the care of those excellent personal physicians: Dr Diet, Dr Quiet, Dr Sunshine and Dr Laughter. And don't forget to take your daily dose of the W-vitamins, water and walking.

Choose the Right Food

One of the doctors you have to consult for a healthy life is Dr Diet. Let me explain: we should choose to eat right – and also for all the right reasons.

We must choose food not only for its texture or taste or its appeal to the palate. We must choose food for its nutritive value and the benefits it will confer on us. Of course, our food should be tasty and pleasant. But that is not its primary purpose. We eat to live – we don't live to eat. Therefore, we must choose foods that enhance life and vitality.

The *Gita* tells us that food is of three types – *sattvic, rajasic* and *tamasic.*

Sattvic foods contributes to inner calm and peace of mind. They induce pious thoughts and feelings. They keep us in a state of emotional poise and equanimity.

Rajasic foods give us plenty of energy – but we spend much of it in digesting and eliminating such food. As it contains energy-enhancers, there is greater likelihood of toxin build-up in the body, if this energy is not fully utilized. Ayurvedic physicians tell us that rich foods in this category generate stress, causing respirative, renal or cardiac disorders. *Rajasic* food also causes obesity, diabetes and ulcers.

Tamasic foods give very little energy and are difficult to digest. They also generate a lot of toxins in the system.

The ideal diet is one that avoids *rajasic* and *tamasic* foods. You will not be surprised to know that what the ancient Hindu scriptures regarded as *sattvic* food is now held up to be the ideal food – although by other names! Experts call it high-fibre, natural, anti-oxidant, etc., and we are encouraged to eat more of such foods. As for what the sages called *rajasic* and *tamasic* food – the very same foods are now labelled high-fat, high-cholestrol, carcinogenic, etc., and we are warned to keep them out of our diets to the greatest extent possible.

In practical terms, food can be of two categories: food of violence or *himsa* – food that includes fish, flesh and fowl;

the alternative is the food of *ahimsa* or non-violence – a vegetarian diet.

During the last fifty years or more, medical experts and nutritionists have largely inclined to the opinion that a vegetarian diet is the best option for good health.

I recommend to my friends that all cooked food should be eaten in moderation; and uncooked food like salads and fresh fruits should be eaten in plenty – I call this my 'sun-cooked' food.

An ancient story tells us that the Angel of Food came before the Divine Presence, battered, exhausted, and severely downcast.

'I can't take it anymore,' he complained. 'People abuse me, exploit me. There is no respect for me – no piety of the realization that I am your *prasadam* to men. Everyone indulges in excess. Never has there been such ill-treatment meted out to one of your gifts.'

The Lord smiled and said to him: 'Those who abuse you and indulge in excess are destroying themselves!'

All diet choices have their consequences. Fast foods fill you up – but they will not sustain your health and vitality. Quick-fix foods that come in packets will give you chemicals and additives – but not much by way of nutrition or good taste.

'Live' foods – fresh, natural fruits and vegetables – add joy and zest to our lives. 'Dead' foods only make your stomach a graveyard for diseased carcasses.

When you choose the right food, you also save yourself a lot of money. Ask yourself what is more expensive – a banana or packet of fried snacks? A bag of tomatoes or a bar of chocolate? A meal of salad and soup or a pizza?

Choose a Healthy Environment

It is in our hands to create a healthy mental and physical environment around us.

Let fresh air and light stream into your homes. Do not shut yourself into air-conditioned or centrally heated cages. If you are forced to work in such an environment, take in as much fresh air and sunlight as you can, through a daily walk in the open air.

Choose a healthy mental environment by dismissing worry, anxiety and negative thoughts out of your life. Choose optimism, positive thoughts, peace and joy.

A happy and congenial living environment contributes to a peaceful, stress-free life. For each of us, this may mean a different scenario. I know that lots of people born and brought up in a crowded but neighbourly and friendly environment of the *peths* and *wadas* of the historic old city of Pune, hated moving to what they regarded as the soulless and alien neighbourhood of the new suburbs and housing societies. Equally, people who hated the din and noise and congestion of the city, did their best to move out to a quiet, modern apartment building as soon as they could afford to do so.

If your work environment is causing stress and anxiety, you should seriously consider switching jobs.

The Lap of Mother Nature

Have you noticed that some of the world's greatest stories of transformation are acted out against the backdrop of magnificent natural scenes? In Shangri-La, on the snowy heights of the Himalayas, a hero finds the secret of eternal bliss. On a mountain peak, yet another discovers the Universal Truth. Amidst the beauty and serenity of the Swiss mountains, Heidi finds her happiness.

Nature is magical; it is mysterious and powerful; it is healing, inspiring and uplifting. The pantheists believe in the godliness of nature. The transcendentalists believe that the spirit of God permeates all of nature. Our own *Isopanishad* tells us: *Ishavasyam Idam Sarvam*, 'All that is, is a vesture of the Lord.'

Nature is a magical healer. When we spend time in the lap of nature, walking in the woods, listening to the music of the birds, tending to our garden or just looking at the evening sky, we feel revitalized. When we breathe in the fresh air of open spaces and unpolluted surroundings, our flagging spirits revive.

Psychologists explain that when we are alone with nature, we let go of our social 'roles' and worldly responsibilities, and therefore connect with the positive forces of the Universe. This is why many people unconsciously choose the seaside or a mountain-resort or an unspoilt natural location as their favourite holiday destination. Nature can heal, inspire and transform. It can work miracles on our tired psyche and exhausted physical frame, and restore us to a sense of harmony and well-being.

Choose the Right Healing

In recent times, medical practitioners have come to acknowledge that diet, environment and the psychological condition of men can influence the immune system and thus affect our health adversely – a weakened immune system leads to a number of illnesses. Thus, several alternative systems of medicine have been able to heal people just by getting them to change their diet, change their environment and their lifestyle.

Consider this: most of us consume excessive carbohydrates and sugars; we are given to the habit of eating junk food; the processed foods we eat contain a lot of harmful chemicals and additives; our homes are cleaned and sprayed with dangerous sprays and insecticides, which play havoc with our immune system.

Turning to holistic medicine can have a beneficial effect on our health. Most of the alternative systems also lay great emphasis on practices like silence, meditation and yoga. These help to cleanse us and rid us from emotional imbalances.

Detoxify Your System!

The environment we live in today is far from healthy. People refer to this planet as a 'toxic world'. The air is polluted; the waters are laden with chemical wastes; even the food we eat is contaminated with pesticides. Perhaps, more people than ever are exposed to toxic overload, causing severe stress to mind and body.

Our systems need to be cleansed and purified to withstand this onslaught and restore the body to its natural balance. But our minds also need the same process of healing and purification. Here are a few tips to detoxify the mind:

- Turn off your TV and switch off your cell phones every now and then
- Negative thoughts act as toxins on your mind – turn them out
- Try to avoid criticizing, judging, resenting other people even in thought
- Burn anger before it burns you
- Avoid the company of negative people
- Spend a few minutes every day in silence
- Develop a new, positive perspective on life

Choose the Right Friends

We all know the old saying: Tell me who your friends are – and I shall tell you what kind of a person you are.

The 'right' people are not the ones who always agree with us. The 'right' people are not the ones who lead us into bad habits. They are not just people who are 'fun' to be with.

The 'right' people are free and frank people who are not afraid to pull you up when you go wrong. They are loyal, courageous people who will stand by you even when things go wrong. They are people who give you moral support and instill self-confidence in you!

Above all, choose to walk the way of truth, integrity and righteousness. We are not all leading heroic or momentous lives: in our own small world, in our own individual lives, let us choose the way of righteousness.

We can – and we must – make the right choices. God has given us the power and the wisdom to do so. We also have the choice to react positively or negatively to everything that appears before us.

The choice is ours!

Exercise

1. *If you were to live your life all over again, what would you choose that is different from the choices you actually made?*
2. *Have you given serious consideration to your lifestyle – the food you eat, your fitness and your attitude to life as a whole?*
3. *What kind of environment suits you, the one that you are happiest in? What have you done to create such an environment at home and at work?*
4. *Have you made the right choice?*

CHAPTER 7

IT'S NOT AS DIFFICULT AS YOU THINK

Sometime ago, a businessman came to meet me. He had suffered a major loss due to the financial misdemeanour of his partner, who also happened to be a friend. He was broken emotionally and physically.

'I trusted my partner completely, Dada,' he said, controlling his feelings with great difficulty. 'I had no reason not to! He was my childhood friend, and his father and my father had been business partners. It never occurred to me that a friend would betray my trust. Tell me, did I choose wrong when I chose to trust him? Is it my fault that my family is now facing a financial catastrophe? Should I have harboured suspicions and kept a close watch on my partner? How will I ever trust my choice again? On what basis will I be able to make further decisions?'

The same kind of anguish was expressed by a couple who met me a few weeks later. They had taken great pains to find a suitable match for their daughter, their only child. They had sifted through many proposals. They had considered family background, social status, financial soundness and inquired thoroughly into the character of the boy. They had made thorough enquiries with friends and family, and consulted the best astrologer to compare the horoscopes of the bride and groom. When they were fully satisfied that it was indeed a suitable match, they went ahead and arranged for a grand wedding.

Imagine their shock and horror when they discovered that the young man had already married his secretary earlier and was the father of a child. Not only were their dreams for their daughter shattered; the girl's life was in ruins.

'We meant well for our daughter, Dada,' wept the mother. 'We wanted nothing but the best for her. We did not make a choice based on our personal bias. We consulted as many people as we could; we spoke to many people who personally knew the family and groom. We had no inkling that it was going to be such a disaster. Where did we go wrong? How can we make amends for our terrible choice?'

Look around you and you are sure to come across many such cases. People make choices in good faith, in the light of their insight and wisdom; and yet things go wrong. Marriages that began as rosy dreams end in divorce; engineering/medical seats 'bought' at a premium by doting fathers are abandoned when their sons decide to pursue their dreams in other directions. Dear ones are entrusted to the care of the best surgeons for a major surgery after positive prognostications and reassurances by doctors and hospital administrators. Though the surgery is successful the patient does not survive! Property, real estate, farmlands bought with lifetime savings turn out to be legal nightmares. The list is endless.

Does all this mean we cannot escape our 'fate' or 'destiny'?

Does this mean our so-called free will is just a myth?

Once again, I assert: God gave us free will and the right to choose. If we choose wrong, even unwittingly, we face the consequences. But in such cases, we must face the effects of our choice in the spirit of humility and acceptance. The wrong choice has been made so that we may learn a few necessary lessons from life. There is little to be gained by blaming ourselves and even less to be gained by blaming God for all our ills. God is too loving to punish; too wise to make a mistake.

Life is full of hard choices. And often we are faced with more than one option. The more the options, the harder it becomes to decide. When there are two options, it is easy to decide which one to take. Get into the lift or climb the staircase. Walk or take a bus. Tea or coffee. Lose your temper or exercise patience. The choice is easy. But if there are more choices, it sometimes becomes difficult to for us to choose right!

In the following pages, I hope to offer you a few practical suggestions on making the right choice. But before I do that, I want to set you in the right frame of mind that will enable you to choose wisely and well.

To be able to make the right choice, you must quieten your mind, calm your senses and open your heart. Clear out all preconceived notions and prejudices. Then invite God into your mind and heart, so that you may receive His grace to decide what is best!

You must practice the presence of God. Practicing the presence means striking a relationship with God. Make God your father, brother or friend. He is your mother too. I tell businessmen to make God their senior partner! Go to God again and again. Talk to God as you would to a relative or a friend. Feel that God is all the time by your side. When the mind wanders, practice the presence by repeating a simple prayer like: 'I love you, God.' Or simply repeat God's name.

The prayer of affirmation also helps when you face a major choice. After carefully considering what are the desirable and undesirable results of the choice you are about to make, think deeply of what you want; and what you don't want out of your choice. Then affirm to yourself: 'Dear God, our lives are safe in Your hands. My children/family/business/life is under Your divine protection. I have no fear for them. I have cast out all fear, for I have surrendered my life into Your safe hands. I know You will take care of my dear ones at every step, every round of life. Please accept my thanks for protecting my dear ones.'

Repeating affirmations are also helpful. You must affirm what you want, not what you don't want. Your affirmation should always be a positive one. There is the law of attraction which states that the universe is a huge copy machine. It does not judge whether your desire is right or wrong. It just draws you closer to what you desire. It has been simply stated, the law of attraction (LOA) is the belief that the universe creates and provides for you that which your thoughts are focussed on. Positive thoughts lead to positive outcomes and persistently negative thoughts lead to negative consequences.

Let me express a few positive affirmations to help you make the right choice:

1. I shall trust and listen to my inner voice.
2. I shall cultivate and cherish loving relationships.
3. I shall change my thinking and change my life.
4. I shall face life with courage.
5. I shall cultivate the attitude of gratitude.
6. I shall practice the virtue of forgiveness that heals myself and others.
7. I shall choose kindness.

*More on these affirmations in the following pages.

POSITIVE AFFIRMATION ONE

I SHALL TRUST AND LISTEN TO MY INNER VOICE

Many a time, when you are looking for answers to difficult questions and solutions to tough problems, you find them within yourself. You just have to be still and listen to your inner voice. The answers are all there for the asking!

The 'inner voice' I speak of is also called 'gut instinct' or 'intuition' or even 'inner guide'. No, I'm not talking about 'hearing' voices, which instruct you to do this or that out of the blue. I'm talking to you about the still, small voice that speaks to you in silence. Men as widely different from each other as the great souled idealist, Gandhiji and the iconic entrepreneur, Steve Jobs, asserted their trust in the inner voice. Gandhiji said, 'Everyone who wills, can hear their inner voice, for it is within everyone.' From his own perspective, Steve Jobs said, 'Your time is limited, so don't waste it living someone else's life. Don't be trapped by dogma – which is living with the results of other people's thinking. Don't let the noise of others' opinions drown out your own inner voice. And most important, have the courage to follow your heart and intuition.'

This inner voice has been interpreted by some as the voice of our conscience or even the voice of divinity within us. It is definitely the voice of our inner wisdom, nurtured by the aggregate of all our life's experiences.

The inner voice is often heard in the mundane, daily workaday world of ours. Have you ever experienced this: you wake up one morning, suddenly thinking about a long lost friend or a dear one with whom you have somehow lost touch; and out of the blue, there is a call or a mail from that person? Have you found yourself going through a routine procedure at work, and all of a sudden you decide to check out a few details and find that you have narrowly escaped from making a faulty decision? My friend, who is a chartered accountant, often tells me that he has a 'sixth sense' telling him something is wrong somewhere, when he opens a spreadsheet to check an account. There are happier instances too, of people recognizing their future life partners the moment they set eyes on him or her for the first time.

Nelson Mandela, the anti-apartheid icon and revolutionary leader who became the President of South Africa and co-winner of the Nobel prize in 1993, was incarcerated in the infamous Robben Island prison to be transferred to other high-security jails for as long as twenty-seven years. During those dark days, when many of his fellow prisoners hovered between hope and despair, Mandela said he found inspiration from a Victorian poem, 'Invictus' by the English poet, William Ernest Henley. A part of the poem is given below:

It matters not how strait the gate,
How charged with punishments the scroll,
I am the master of my fate:
I am the captain of my soul.

Nelson Mandela not only read the full poem, he would often recite it to his fellow prisoners to encourage them and empower their struggle for the cause of freedom. If Mandela's spirit triumphed over adversity and chose the path of hope over despair, it was because he listened to his inner voice. 'I always knew that someday I would once again feel the grass under my feet and walk in the sunshine as a free man,' he would say later.

Invictus as a poem has an interesting background story. In 1875, the poet Henley was told that one of his legs had to be amputated due to complications arising from tuberculosis. As bad luck would have it, soon after the amputation surgery was carried out, doctors told him that his other leg would also have to go in order to save his life. The poet faced a tough choice; allow the surgeons to amputate his one remaining leg, and choose life over death.

Henley made a courageous choice, he decided to consult the distinguished English surgeon Joseph Lister, who was actually able to save Henley's remaining leg after multiple surgical interventions on the foot. The poem, his only known composition, was written during this period of adversity and pain.

How can you access your inner voice and gain the wisdom to make the right choice? Here are certain preconditions that you must fulfil:

1. Ask yourself what you really want from a particular situation. What is it that will make you truly happy? What are the effects/consequences that will make you very unhappy?
2. Consider the effects of your choice on your loved ones and other people around you. How will your decision affect them?
3. The third and most important question which counsellors and mentors often ask is, 'Do you want to be right, or do you want to be happy?' In other words, set a clear conscience and your peace of mind above all other goals you may have and organize all other goals around it.

May I add that you can never get to hear that still small voice inside you unless you learn to practice silence? There are millions of us who do not know what it is to go into silence, even briefly! They may be all alone, in perfect solitude; but the clamour of their thoughts and feelings drown the inner voice. Getting to know yourself, understanding your true nature and realizing what you really want out of life is a long, exploratory process. It does not happen in a flash. Reflection, meditation and silence open the doors to the inner recesses of your heart, which you have neglected to take charge of, in the hustle and bustle of life. Our excuse is that we have no time! We have no time to get to know ourselves, let alone to understand and cherish the best part of our true self.

The point is that no one can teach you the goal of your life. It is only your own inner voice which can tell you what you should do with your life.

Always cherish the still, small voice within you. It is a soft, inner voice which is likely to be drowned in the shout and clamour of the big, bad world. It is up to us to ensure that it is always kept alert, alive and sharp. Do not allow the voice of your inner divinity to be extinguished – as it is your guide to right thinking and living.

The incident with which I am going to conclude this chapter is no ordinary story. It is the climactic moment of what has been called 'the greatest story ever told'. It is the story of Jesus Christ's final hours as a free man before the terrible events of his arrest and trial by the Romans. We must remember that Jesus too, faced a crucial choice, that night in the Mount of Olives.

According to the Gospels, Jesus went with three of his disciples to the Garden of Gethsemane. He exhorted his disciples to pray, while he himself moved 'a stone's throw away' from them; he felt a sense of overwhelming sadness and anguish, and prayed, 'My Father, if it is possible, let this cup pass me by. Nevertheless, let it be as you, not I, would have it.'

A little while later, He said, 'If this cup cannot pass by, but I must drink it, your will be done.' (Matthew 26:42). He said this prayer not once, not twice, but three times, checking on the three apostles between each prayer and finding them asleep. He commented, 'The spirit is willing, but the flesh is weak'. We are told that an angel came from heaven to strengthen him. During his agony as he prayed, 'his sweat was as it were great drops of blood falling down upon the ground'. (Luke 22:44).

At the conclusion of his silent communion with God, Jesus accepts that the hour has come for him to fulfil his destiny; he chooses to embrace the will of God and face what life has in store for him.

Some of you may be staggered, overwhelmed by this story. You will undoubtedly protest, 'But Jesus was the son of God! He could face the choice of life and martyrdom! We are lesser mortals.'

But that is just the point. If Jesus needed silence and reflection and communion with his inner Divinity before he faced his crucial choice, don't we need to follow his divine example in deeds of our daily life?

Exercise

1. *Have you ever felt an inner 'hunch' or urge to take a particular decision?*

2. *Are you an 'intuitive' person?*
3. *When you try to reflect before making a crucial decision, do your own doubts and qualms drown out the voice of your inner guidance?*
4. *Do you practice silence in your daily life?*

POSITIVE AFFIRMATION TWO

I SHALL CULTIVATE AND CHERISH LOVING RELATIONSHIPS

A loving relationship is one of the most valuable assets we can be blessed with.

We ensure that our money, our precious jewels, our movable and immovable assets are secure and well-protected. But I wonder how far we value something that is our greatest asset in this worldly life, namely human relationships.

As human beings, there are quite a lot of people and things that we relate to: we cherish mother nature and the environment we live in; we develop a special attachment to certain locations like our favourite parks, beaches or mountains; we have special nooks and quiet places within and outside our homes; there are also certain times of the day that are special to us. In fact, we have a vital working relationship with so many of these treasured places and times. Our peaceful morning walk, our quiet ten minutes on the terrace or the balcony, our comfortable stretch on that cozy rocking chair.

But human relationships are special. They need to be nourished, sustained, carefully cultivated, so that they don't wither away due to our neglect. However, if there is one other thing we take for granted in life apart from the air we breathe, it is those very relationships that make our life meaningful. We choose our cherished relationships carefully enough to begin with: but having made them, we choose to allow most of them to thrive on benign neglect.

I used the term 'benign neglect' because the moment anyone reminds you of the special people in your life, most of you will protest that you love them beyond all else. 'Of course, I love my parents,' swears the married man who lives a thousand miles away from home and is totally immersed in his career/business/family/finances. 'Naturally, my siblings will always be special to me,' says the brother or sister, who has made it a habit to call up siblings every New Year (their birthdays having been long forgotten.)

Relationships are not confined to family alone, though to most of us, families must always come first. But I would like you to think of the larger human family today: of friends, friends-in-the-making, colleagues at work, neighbours, and the hundreds of people whose lives you touch one way or the other.

The interconnectedness of human beings is one of the most beautiful things in life; let me give you the beautiful words of the original sermon by John Donne, from the book *Devotions upon Emergent Occasions*:

> No man is an island entire of itself; every man is a piece of the continent, a part of the main . . . And therefore never send to know for whom the bell tolls; it tolls for thee.

Ask yourself: do you value these precious human relationships? Do you take pain to nourish and cherish them?

Never send to know for whom the bell tolls; it tolls for thee.

Today, nearly 600 years after the sermon was delivered, people hold it up as an exemplary warning against isolation and indifference. No one suffers alone, the poet argues emphatically; and being aware of another's pain and suffering only makes us stronger, more sensitive, and more caring.

Human relationships are at once subtle, delicate and complex. They need to be nurtured and strengthened, healed and cherished, as much as the people involved in them. When the going is good, everything is smooth and hassle-free, loving warmth and affection, friendship and understanding flourish. But when things begin to go wrong, the ride becomes rough. The human tendency is to shift the blame, accuse the other person and assume the role of the injured party, and, in general, feel that one is the victim and the other is the culprit. This happens to everyone, at one time or another in life – between parents and children, husband and wife, siblings and friends, and partners and colleagues.

I often tell my friends, the greatest famine in the world today is the famine of understanding. No two people seem to understand each other these days. Therefore, misunderstandings abound in our lives. There is misunderstanding in our homes, clubs, schools, colleges, universities, corporations and organizations.

I recall the words of the great Parsi Prophet, Zoroaster: 'Know well that a hundred temples of wood and stone have not the value of one understanding heart!' Understanding hearts are what we need, so that people may cultivate and cherish loving relationships that are the elixir of human life!

Pause and think for a minute: how have you chosen to treat your relationship with the people who matter most in your life?

Relationships are for cherishing; not for criticizing, fault finding and playing a blame game. And the best way to nourish relationships is by making an effort to understand people, putting yourself in their shoes, empathizing with them, and appreciating their presence in your life.

Today, most people view relationships negatively: think of the familiar complaints you hear in every direction. My parents don't understand me/ My children don't appreciate what I do for them/My husband can't spare out time for me/ My wife doesn't realize the stress I face every day/ My staff is no good/ My superior is very harsh, and so on and so forth.

For a change, shall we choose the following positive assertions just for today?

- I am lucky to have parents who are so supportive . . .
- My children make my life worthwhile . . .
- Life is beautiful because of my friends . . .
- I'm glad to be working and happy to be part of a team . . .
- Where would I be without all of them who make my life what it is?
- I value all the people in my life . . . the domestic helpers, the office assistants, the shopkeepers who serve me, the civic workers who keep the city and the traffic and the systems moving . . . Where would I be without their unseen presence?

Choose to cherish your precious relationships. Learning to value people, learning to appreciate them is the first step to establishing successful relationships. So-called 'incompatibilities' and 'misunderstandings' have to be resolved through continual effort, understanding and reconciliation – by a constant process of loving and forgiving, give and take, understanding and empathy. There is no such thing as a broken bond; there are only misunderstandings and mistakes, which can easily be set right if we have the will to do so.

Let us choose here and now, to understand and appreciate the people in our lives; let us learn to listen; let us learn to put ourselves in the other person's shoes before we find fault or criticize them.

When you make a difficult choice, when you confront a difficult decision, don't just consider what is in it for you! Think of the people who will be affected by your choice: your family, friends, subordinates, neighbours and business associates.

Treat your spouse as an equal partner, however difficult it may be in this patriarchal society in which we live. Respect his/her feelings and aspirations and do not treat your partner as a convenient adjunct to your life.

When you make choices for your children, take their dreams and aspirations into consideration. While it may be perfectly normal for parents to choose a good kindergarten or primary school for their kids, it is up to the children to decide whether they want to play tennis or hockey, to learn to swim or play the guitar, and to choose engineering, medicine or hotel management as a career. Imposing your views and dreams on them (even if your parents did it to you) is going to be counterproductive! I give you the words of Kahlil Gibran:

> Your children are not your children.
> They are the sons and daughters of Life's longing for itself.
> They come through you but not from you,
> And though they are with you yet they belong not to you . . .

Choose to give your children wings. Don't expect them to be surrogate players who are there to fulfil your dreams.

As for the children, I would tell them: offer love and respect to the parents who gave you life and brought you up; live life on your own terms, but do not fail to give your parents a special place in your hearts and homes.

If you are fortunate enough to have family elders, grandparents, learn to love and cherish them! Recent research carried out by psychologists at Emory University tells us that children who know firsthand about their family history (having heard about their parents and their families from their grandparents, including details of where they came from, where they went to school, how the family made or lost its fortune, how the uncles and aunts grew up, etc.) always proved to be more resilient and positive than children brought up in isolation. This kind of family knowledge builds what psychologists call 'the inter generational self', or the sense that the children feel themselves belonging to something larger than their individual selves!

Recently, I read this story about a young man who successfully cleared three levels of interviews and was scheduled to meet the MD of the company for a final round. The young man's academic record was so brilliant that the MD asked him if he has availed of government scholarships in school or University. The candidate replied, 'No sir, never.'

'Was it your father who paid for your education throughout?'

'I lost my father when I was barely three years old, sir. It was my mother who worked to put me through school and college.'

'Where did she work?' asked the MD. The young man replied that she had worked (and was still working) as a clothes cleaner and laundry woman in a boarding house.

The MD asked to see the young man's hands; he saw that they were clean and soft and well-groomed. 'Have you ever washed clothes for your mother?' he asked the young man. 'No sir, never,' the son replied. 'My mother would never allow it; she would tell me to go back to my books and study well.'

'Alright,' said the MD. 'Tonight when you go home, I'd like you to look closely at your mother's hands and clean them. When we meet tomorrow morning, I'd like you to tell me what you felt.'

The young man was excited. He felt that he was sure to get the job. He rushed home and said to his mother, who was busy washing clothes, 'Mom, let me look at your hands.'

The mother was taken aback by this sudden request. Half crying and half happy, her mixed emotions starting to show in the form of tears, she held out her hands and her son felt them. He found her hands wrinkled and rough with bruises and callouses. His tears flowing copiously, he washed and cleaned them, and told his mother to rest, while he washed the remaining clothes.

Next morning, when he met the MD, he was in a sombre and subdued frame of mind. 'So tell me, did you go home and clean your mother's hands?' asked the senior officer. 'Tell me what you felt?'

The young man looked up at the MD, and the executive saw that his eyes were filled with tears. 'I wish I could accurately describe to you my feelings. The first thing I felt was appreciation for all the effort and pain my mother put in to make me what I am. The second was the realization that nothing in life ever comes to us on a platter; there is someone's hard work and sacrifice behind every achievement. The third was overwhelming gratitude for family relationships. I made my mother rest and washed clothes for her. We spent a lot of time talking about our past, and the tough and difficult life she had. I am so grateful to you for this sir. I have always loved my mother; but now, I value her as a wonderful human being.'

The senior executive said to him, 'You are hired as a manager in this company. I need someone who can appreciate the work of others, respect hard work and be grateful for the help he receives from others. Money and profit making alone are not the goals of this company. We need to work as a team and respect each other.'

Exercise

1. *Think of your close relationships. Is there anything that disturbs you or upsets you about them?*
2. *Who do you think is to blame? You or the other person involved?*
3. *Try to let go of all resentments and resolve to change yourself and your attitude so that the relationship can be mended.*
4. *Choose to cherish your precious relationships!*

POSITIVE AFFIRMATION THREE

I SHALL CHANGE MY THINKING AND CHANGE MY LIFE

In a world obsessed by negatives – strife, controversy, discord among nations; misunderstanding, hostility and conflict between people; tension, depression and frustration within individuals, I give you the message of optimism and faith that I have always believed in, 'Happiness is your birthright, as a child of God.'

No, we cannot change circumstances at will; but we can change our attitude to circumstances. And I firmly believe: you are not a failure until you give up trying. You cannot be defeated, except from within. There is no insurmountable barrier except your own weakness. There is no problem that you and God cannot handle together.

This, therefore, is one of the crucial choices you must make: cultivate the right attitude. Change your thinking – and change your life.

You may ask: isn't this a bit far-fetched? How can thinking change my life? How can it change the world around me, which is the cause of all my problems?

David started smoking on the sly when he was fourteen years old. By the time he was twenty-five, he was smoking forty cigarettes a day. When his aunt, a cancer specialist, spoke to him earnestly and invited him to attend a lecture on 'Smoking Kills', he decided to turn over a new leaf. He decided to quit smoking. It was not easy. But with tremendous will power and determination, he succeeded.

It was barely two years since Vijay started working; a little over six months since his marriage. He ran up a credit card bill of twenty lakh rupees, including interest. His father-in-law, a businessman, stepped in to save him from accumulating debt and dishonour. But his wife was so mortified she walked out of the marriage. Vijay underwent a course in mind control and with a marathon effort, broke out of the habit of compulsive spending. A year later, his life was back on track and he and his wife got back together after counselling.

David and Vijay made life-changing decisions after having made the wrong choice initially.

'Men's natures are alike; it is their habits that separate them,' said Confucius. Positive thinking can work for you if you put your mind to it.

Researchers in psychology tell us that on an average, the common man has around 60,000–90,000 thoughts passing through his mind every day: and out of these, more than ninety-six per cent of thoughts are the same ones you thought the day before! In other words, despite our continuous thinking, only four per cent per day are new thoughts. You keep thinking the same thing: well, I shall have a couple of cigarettes, and I will feel clearer in my mind. Or, I shall go out and buy something for myself and that will make me feel better. Or, I was born fat and I shall die fat; I'm unfit any way and it's not going to be possible to lose all that weight; I might as well eat whatever I like.

You think the same old tired thoughts; you start believing them yourself; you act on those beliefs and your life becomes troubled: excessive smoking/excessive spending/ excessive weight. You need to avoid those deadly thought traps.

Let me hasten to add: there's hardly anyone among us who has not had to deal with negative thinking patterns at one time or another in our lives. Please do not make the mistake of imagining that you are the only one with such destructive thinking. Negative thinking comes to all normal people; only we have to learn to deal with it effectively.

Let the negative thoughts perish! But don't stop with putting the negatives out of your mind; replace them with positive thoughts. In the words of the Bible, 'Finally, brothers and sisters, whatever is true, whatever is noble, whatever is right, whatever is pure, whatever is lovely, whatever is admirable –

if anything is excellent or praiseworthy – think about such things . . .' [Philippians 4:8]

Thoughts are forces; thoughts can influence our actions and change our personalities; thoughts are the building blocks of our life. A thought, if it is constantly held in the mind, will drive us to action. An action, which is repeated, creates a habit. The sum total of our habits forms our character, which determines our destiny. Therefore, if we wish to change our destiny, we must begin with the thought. Change the pattern of your thinking – and you can change your life for the better!

Let me explain this to you with a small example. A young lady returns home after a tough day at the office. She is mentally and physically exhausted. Her back is aching; her head is splitting; she can't face food. All she wants to do is take a hot bath and collapse on her bed.

Then the phone rings. It is from her best friend who has just come back from a holiday abroad. The friend wants to meet her and take her out to a five-star hotel for a special dinner party. And she has got such exciting gifts which she wants to hand over as soon as possible. Can she please come over?

The girl is galvanized into action. In a jiffy she is bathed, spruced, dressed, made-up, perfumed and looking like a million dollars. She zips out of the house to meet up with her friend and spends an exciting evening; she returns home late at night, loaded with presents which she opens and admires not once but several times. And when she goes to bed, she can't sleep for her sheer excitement.

Choose the right attitude, the positive attitude. Everything changes when your attitude changes. Your attitude controls your body. When the girl's attitude was negative, her mind signalled weariness and exhaustion to the body. 'I'm tired!' The body began to respond to the message with sluggishness. It began to believe that it needed to collapse, it could not carry on. Her entire metabolism had slowed down, accepting the message of the mind.

A phone call changed her weariness to excitement. Her mind was filled with enthusiasm. She was ready to go out, meet her friend, catch up with all the news and share a lovely meal with her! Her emotions were now singing a different tune. 'Hurry, Hurry!' She got her strength, energy, vitality and a sparkle. She was ready for anything now!

It is a clinically-proven fact that your body reacts to your attitude. I know bankers and financiers who suffered a heart-attack when their investments proved to be bad. Equally, I have known chronically ill patients revive miraculously when a marriage is announced or a baby is born in the family. Bad news can make you ill; and good news can make you well. Negative emotions create an imbalance in your body, leading to ill-health; positive emotions restore the balance, bringing good health. Your body reacts to your attitude and changes your state of health. If you wish to change your life, you only have to change your attitude. You can only change your attitude and choose to be healthy.

There are people who focus their attention only on problems and difficulties. Tell them of your dreams and plans, and they will say, 'No! It is impossible! It will never work.' They will point out all the drawbacks and weaknesses in your plan, and try their best to convince you that you cannot win. These are the people who can boast, 'Bring me a solution and I will give you a problem.'

David W. Hartman of Pennsylvania became blind when he was eight-year-old. He had always dreamt of studying medicine; but the medical school to which he applied for admission discouraged him severely by pointing out that no one with visual disability had ever completed a medical course. Hartman refused to be negative. Courageously, he took on the task of 'reading' by having twenty-five medical textbooks audio-recorded for him. At twenty-seven, David W. Hartman became the first blind student to complete medical school.

There were two men who came to a rehabilitation centre for the disabled. Each one of them had lost an arm.

At the end of one-year's training, one of them was so discouraged that he came to the conclusion that life was not worth living with the kind of deformity he had.

The other man was so joyful that he went about saying that it was a boon that nature had given people two arms, when he could get along perfectly well with just one.

Positive thinking cannot be taught, it must be caught. Therefore, be careful of the company you keep. If you move in the company of positive-minded people, their positive vibrations and energy will influence you to develop an optimistic spirit.

The second thing that will help you develop positive thinking is to count your blessings. There was a woman whose friend asked her if she counted sheep to fall asleep. The woman replied, 'I don't count sheep, I count my blessings instead. I count them up to a point where I don't need to number them anymore. Then I just relax and know that God is in charge, and will take care of me from anything, present or future.'

If there is one choice we all must make, it is to choose the right thinking, the right attitude.

Adopt a positive attitude to life. This cannot be done in a day. But you must begin now. Never put off for tomorrow, what you can do today. Never put off for later, what you can do right away.

No one outside of us can harm us. It is only we who harm ourselves. It is very easy to lay the blame at the door of another. It is so easy to say, 'It's only because of A or B that I am in trouble now.' But the truth is, no one outside of us has this power. It was a wise woman who said, 'The longer I live, the more convinced I become, that life is ten per cent what happens to us and ninety per cent how we respond to it.' Add to this the statement, 'Attitude is more important than education, bank balance, influence, position and power and the circumstances in which we are in now. If we change our attitude, we can change our lives.'

When attitudes are right, there is no barrier we cannot cross, no dream we cannot realize, no goals we cannot achieve, no challenges we cannot overcome. It was John Miller who said:

'Your living is determined not so much by what life brings to you, as by the attitude you bring to life.'

A few years ago I was in Delhi, when I was invited by *Doordarshan* to visit their studio. There I met a wonderful man. He had lost both his arms in an accident. But he had a positive attitude. He trained his feet so that he could take up the job of composing in a press. With a smile on his face and a feeling of joy, he said, 'I earn ₹500 a month. I am not a burden on anyone.'

There was another man whom I met in Pune. He was sitting by the wayside, and he had lost both his legs.

'What happened to you?' I asked him.

'Nothing,' he replied. 'I was born this way.'

'May I ask, who takes care of you, my friend?'

'My mother – and above all, God.'

'Do you find it difficult, inconvenient to move about?'

'Do you find it difficult and inconvenient that you don't have wings?' he asked me. 'Don't you think it would be far better if you could fly on your own, rather than waiting to catch planes?'

'Life is a matter of habit,' he continued. 'If you start complaining, there is so much to complain about. It is the attitude that counts.'

The following steps will help you cultivate a positive attitude:

- Empty your mind of all negative thoughts and fill it with fresh, invigorating, positive thoughts. Set aside time everyday, to give your mind a good shampoo.

- An expert tailor says that the best way to keep clothes in good shape is to make sure that the pockets are emptied when they are hung up. We may infer from this, that the best way to keep ourselves and our lives in good shape is to empty our minds of all worries, anxieties, tensions and negative thoughts before we retire for the night. We can then begin the new day with energy, vigour and freshness.
- Whenever your mind is driving you towards negative thinking, affirm to yourself positive thoughts that will change the track of your thinking.
- The world's scriptures are full of dynamic, positive energetic thoughts, which have the power to boost your morale and keep your spirits high. Choose any thought that appeals to you and repeat it to yourself constantly.

The great psychiatrist, Karl Menninger, has said: 'Think big. Men do not break down because they are defeated, but only because they think they are.' Do not think defeat; think victory. Think big, act big, believe big, pray big. This is the formula to overcome tension.

A world famous shoe manufacturer took a decision to expand his business by setting up a new branch in a remote, little-known country. He called up one of his marketing managers and asked him to take the next flight to the country and explore the possibility of setting up a new factory there.

The young executive flew out the very next day. But within twenty-four-hours of reaching there, he called up his boss. 'This place is not good for our business,' he said gloomily. 'People do not wear shoes out here. We'd better forget any notion of setting up a factory here. It simply won't do. And I am catching the next flight home.'

The boss was highly dissatisfied with the report. He had set his heart on doing what he wanted. So he called up another young manager and sent him out with the same order.

Within a few hours of landing there, the young man called up in great excitement. 'This place is unbelievable,' he exclaimed. 'Our business will experience a boom here. These people don't even know what shoes are like. When we introduce shoes here, we shall have a whole, new, untapped market. Send in our planners and architects as soon as you can. We must set up a factory here and we shall win all the way.'

What a difference a positive attitude can make!

Have you heard the beautiful story about the six-year old girl who found out that she was adopted by her parents, whom she loved more than anything else in the world? The child was stunned by the discovery. 'I'm not your own baby, am I?' she kept asking. 'You didn't make me, you only took me.'

Her mother was a sensitive woman. She said to her daughter, 'Well darling, people just get their own children, and they don't have a choice in the matter. But you are special because we actually chose you.'

In a research on working women, it was found that even among those doing the same kind of jobs, some people viewed work as a series of hassles, while others saw it as a positive experience in which they were in control of their lives. Among those who felt positive about their work, satisfaction was thirty per cent higher.

If you would see your work only as a 'job' then it drags you down. If you see it as a calling, a vocation, then it is no longer toil or trouble. It becomes an expression of your 'self', a part of you.

A distinguished visitor arrived at a quarry where several poor labourers were toiling hard. He went up to a few of them and asked just one question of each man: 'What are you doing?'

The first one snarled angrily, 'Can't you see I am breaking stones?'

The second one wiped the sweat off his brow and replied, 'I am earning a living to feed my wife and children.'

The third man looked up at him and said cheerfully, 'I am helping to build a beautiful temple.'

You can imagine which of these men got the most out of his work.

Whether you are at home, or in the workplace or among friends, you must exude optimism and positive thinking – and you will find it reflected right back at you.

If you are facing a challenge – trying to win a game or just finish a difficult assignment, what kind of people would you like to have with you? Negative people who keep telling you that you will fail – or positive people who motivate you to succeed?

We always gravitate towards optimists who expect the best out of life. Living a happy, contented life is a great challenge –

and a great achievement. It is a challenge that is best met with optimism.

Yasa was the son of a rich nobleman, and lived in a palace. Coming under the influence of the Buddha, he renounced all his wealth and comfort and accepted all the hardships of a mendicant's life. He slept on the bare ground. He ate what he received as alms from charitable people. He was happy.

One day, he got a severe attack of rheumatism. At first, he took the pain in his stride. Days passed by: the pain persisted. He could not walk with ease. At times the pain was so great that he could not even concentrate on his meditation. He felt miserable; gone was the joy of his life. His mind became sluggish; he felt weary and exhausted.

One day, as he was out begging alms, he found a little girl playing with her friends. She was a cripple; she had but one leg and was hobbling on crutches. Yet, she was happy as a wave dancing on the sea! She shouted and laughed and made merry with the other children.

Seeing her, Yasa felt ashamed of himself. 'This little girl who has only one leg is bright and happy,' he said to himself. 'And I, a disciple of the Buddha, am dejected by a little pain.' He turned over a new leaf. The pain could no longer trouble him. He was free.

Depression is not due to what happens to us: it is due to what happens within us. Choose to be a new you from the inside!

Exercise

1. *Do you often use negative words/expressions in your conversation? (eg. This can't be done, it's impossible, I can't make it, etc?) If you think the answer is yes, switch to more positive words and expressions like 'Yes, I can,' 'Sure, it will be done,' etc.*
2. *How often do you think good things about yourself and others? Look out for things and facts and circumstances to be positive about. Find out things about yourself and others which you like.*
3. *How often do you smile? Smiling automatically puts you in a positive frame of mind.*
4. *Choose to think positive!*

POSITIVE AFFIRMATION FOUR

I SHALL FACE LIFE WITH COURAGE

Life demands of us that we live with courage. Winston Churchill considered courage to be the greatest of all virtues – because we cannot exhibit any other virtue without it. Without the courage to act, justice would be impossible. Without the courage to love, compassion and understanding would not exist. Without the courage to endure, faith and hope would not flourish.

Linguistic experts relate the English word courage to the French word *coeur*, meaning heart. Courage is born of the heart. It is the heart's response to the impulse of fear.

Tagore's immortal hymn begins with the words:

Where the mind is without fear . . .

The *Bhagavad Gita* tells us:

Meet the transient world
With neither grasping nor fear,
Trust the unfolding of life
And you will attain true serenity.

The uncertainties of life have to be taken on, faced with courage. Escape and running away are no solutions.

Whenever I am travelling abroad, people ask me why we do not observe Mother's Day in India. My reply to them is, 'Everyday is Mother's Day in India.' Indeed, where would we be without our mothers? Mothers are our unsung heroes. Every day, they bravely take on the task of feeding, clothing and taking care of their children and families. They walk them to school; help them with their homework. They wash and iron; they cook and clean. They balance budgets, they plan for the future. They participate in community activities, they observe festivals, fasts and holy days. Their work never stops. Yet, how many of us appreciate their courage?

Courage is the key. To live a full life, to live according to God's plan, to live life purposefully and meaningfully, requires courage.

For those of us who live by our faith, as well as those who place their belief on 'science', life poses a series of unanswered – at times unanswerable – questions. Why do bad things happen to good people? Why did a young, intelligent man, husband, father, brother and son to a family of wonderful people have to die of a rare, unheard form of cancer? Why are beautiful young babies sometimes born blind or deformed or spastic? Why are the nations of this world piling up a nuclear arsenal that can destroy the planet ten times over?

Truly, it has been said, to be sentenced to life is to be sentenced to death. Therefore it is said, cowards die several deaths.

Life is full of uncertainties, the unknown and the unknowable. Experts recommend that we develop what they call, 'a high tolerance for uncertainty' if we are to live in peace, even while being aware that so much in our lives is outside our control. Losing control, living with uncertainty generates fear and this fear can be conquered by the right attitude – by loving kindness, faith and compassion.

It was a wise thinker who pointed out that there are two great sources of power, two great forces of strength in this world: one of them is vested in those who are not afraid to kill, hurt, wound, maim and destroy; the other is vested in those who are not afraid to love, forgive, heal and be reconciled.

Yes, we must be unafraid to love – for it requires courage. I have always believed that the power of love is far greater than the power of hatred. If we are to confront the dark forces of destruction and annihilation, we must use the greatest weapon in our possession – the power of love.

Let us admit: it is not as if we face life-and-death situations which require raw, physical courage. But there are difficult challenges life throws at us out of nowhere. A mother of two is told that she has to have an emergency surgery; the only earning member and head of a family is told that he is facing a lay-off; someone is told that he may have contracted a life-threatening illness; or it may be that you are simply surrounded by people who constantly irritate you and get on your nerves.

The important thing under such circumstances, is to face the world with courage and make the right choice. Even under the most difficult of circumstances, courage is a choice, which transforms our tragedies into triumphs.

When I talk of making the right choice with courage, under trying circumstances, I can only recall the tough decision that my Master had to make in the terrible years after the partition of India.

For many Sindhis, the historic event of the nation's freedom meant the loss of their homeland. The Hindus of Sind felt that if they were to be true to the faith of their fathers, they could no longer stay in their homeland. Leaving their properties and possessions behind, they bade farewell to the soil of their birth and sought new homes in India. While most migrated to India only to get into cramped and overcrowded refugee camps, others chose to settle in distant parts of the world, where families and friends had established roots. True, Punjab and Bengal were also partitioned; but Punjabi and Bengali refugees from Pakistan still had a homeland, a home state in India where their language and culture continued unchanged. Unfortunately, for the Sindhi Hindus, there was no place they could call home; no 'space' to call their own in geographical, cultural, and linguistic terms. This is a state of affairs that continues to this day. Sind had gone entirely to Pakistan.

Indian independence was hailed by many as a 'triumph of non-violence'. A 'bloodless revolution' was supposed to have taken place. Alas, the orgies of murder, which came in the wake of freedom, broke even the heart of the great apostle of non-violence, Mahatma Gandhi. The happenings of those days – organized loot and plunder, arson and killing in broad daylight – are a blot on the fair name of our ancient, unhappy land.

To start with, in the early days, Sadhu Vaswani and a small group of his followers remained in Sind for a little over a year after the partition. The Master felt he should stay on, and that the St Mira's Schools should continue to serve the children of those who had newly arrived in Sind. However, prevailing circumstances compelled them to leave the land of their birth.

In that dark period, utter lawlessness prevailed in the cultured cradle of civilization that Sind had always been, a land where Hindus, Muslims and Sikhs had lived side by side in peace and harmony. Cut-throats and assassins, murderers and looters roamed the land freely. An unruly mob took it into their heads to try and 'capture' St Mira's High School and a storm of vilification and vicious propaganda was raised. At a meeting of about 30,000 people, the lie was spread, that at the time of Mr. Jinnah's death, *halwa* had been distributed at Sadhu Vaswani's satsang. In reality, what had actually been distributed was the *kadah prasad* of the satsang. But the incensed mob, who were not prepared to listen or understand, cheered a mob leader who declared loudly, with a pistol in his hand, 'This Vaswani shall not live.'

The editor of a local daily paper came to meet me and narrated the whole incident. 'It is for me to warn you, dear Jashan,' he said. 'It is for you to see that Sadhu Vaswani does not move out for a few days.' Then, with a twinkle in his eyes, he added, 'See that you broach the matter with Sadhu Vaswani very tactfully.'

Experience had taught me, however, not to use 'tact' in dealing with the Master. So, when he got ready for the usual evening walk, I narrated all that I had heard and entreated the Master, 'I pray, Dada, that you keep indoors for a few days. For ought I to know, the man may be prowling somewhere near, looking out for a chance to use his pistol.'

Sadhu Vaswani only smiled. He said to me, 'My child! Remember one thing. Life is a gift of God. What He hath given, only He can take away. When it be His Will, this body will mingle with the dust. And when that moment arrives, no power on earth can hold me back. Until the hour hath come, no pistol-shot can touch a single hair of my head. Blessed be His Name!'

But alas, in November 1948, one of the members of Sadhu Vaswani's satsang was brutally murdered. The Master became anxious for the safety of those who stayed on in Pakistan just because of him. He finally decided to leave Hyderabad–Sind, the city of his birth, and move to India, where he could continue with his humanitarian work. We flew to Bombay on the 10 November 1948.

As I said earlier, I can never forget the first few years following the partition of India, when I spent much of my time accompanying my Master, Gurudev Sadhu Vaswani on visits to refugee camps in India. I cannot tell you the put it together rending spectacle of deprivation, poverty and suffering that we encountered among our brothers and sisters, who were now homeless refugees. In one stroke, they had lost homes, lands, employment, material goods and, for many, even loved ones. Sadhu Vaswani urged them to be strong within. He exhorted them to be self-sufficient and refrain from begging for government help. Again and again, he repeated those magic words, which became a mantra of positive thinking for all his followers: 'Within you lies a hidden *shakti*; awaken that *shakti* and all will be well with you.'

True to his words, the displaced Sindhi community rebuilt their shattered lives and rose like a phoenix from the ashes to become one of the world's most prosperous and philanthropic society. To this day, the Sindhis remain a highly cultured and civilized people – enterprising, hardworking, industrious, full of business acumen, enthused by the spirit of faith and courage. Every Sindhi can be proud of the fact that he belongs to a philanthropic community with a global presence, ever ready to offer a hand of fellowship and friendship to people, wherever they are. The Sindhis faced adversity and misfortune with fortitude and resilience. They had the courage to never give up. They had the courage to make the right choice.

Exercise

1. *Identify those areas of your life where you need courage to take firm decisions.*
2. *Do you think you will develop the will power and courage to act in those areas?*
3. *What do you think you can do to become courageous in thought, word, and deed?*
4. *Choose to live with courage!*

POSITIVE AFFIRMATION FIVE

I SHALL CULTIVATE THE ATTITUDE OF GRATITUDE

Let me begin with this passage (author unknown) that a friend sent to me:

> Be thankful . . .
>
> It's easy to be thankful for the good things. A life of rich fulfilment comes to those who are also thankful for the setbacks. Gratitude can turn a negative into a positive. Find a way to be thankful for your troubles, and they can become your blessings.

When you have more than one option to choose from, thank God!

When you take a decision based on your instinct and intelligence, ask God to bless your decision and thank God for the freedom you have been given to choose.

When things go well for you after you have made the decision, thank God.

When things don't go as you expected and the consequences are difficult, thank God and ask Him to bless you with the wisdom and courage to handle the situation.

Always repeat. 'Thank you, God!'

Friends who have heard me speak or read any of my books know that this is my favourite form of communication with God. In sunshine and rain, in pain and gain, in darkness and light, this is a prayer that I love to offer to God. I say this to Him in all circumstances and all events of life. I say it with the fullest confidence that whatever is happening to me at this moment, is a gift, *prasadam*, from His stainless hands.

As I said to you, this is my favourite prayer but many of our brothers and sisters with whom I have shared this prayer are not convinced by my poor words. 'Thank God?' they ask, incredulous with anger and frustration. 'Thank God? For what? Inflation and recession? Debts and mounting bills? For the cruelty and indifference we experience wherever we turn? For illness and pain?'

I say to them with a smile, 'I know that life is not always smooth sailing for us human beings. But I do know that God is all love and all-knowing. He is too loving to punish and too wise to make a mistake. Whatever is happening to you must be for your own good, though you may not be aware of it when it is happening. Therefore, I say to you, let the words, 'Thank you, God, Thank you, God, Thank you, God,' constantly be on your lips. A grateful heart will make your life beautiful and abundantly blessed.'

As for that question, 'What is there to be grateful about?' I must confess that it leaves me speechless with disbelief. 'What is there that I need not be grateful for?' is my response. As for me, I am grateful to be alive; I am grateful that I can see and hear and feel. Let me add for your sake: you must be grateful that you can walk and run. After seven years of restricted movement following a stroke, I am profoundly grateful that I can come to the *satsang* and meet my brothers and sisters. I also express my gratitude to the doctors, nurses, physiotherapists who helped with my healing, and the numerous brothers and sisters who sent out their prayers for my recovery. I cannot, at present, walk without help; as for running, it is out of question. But I am grateful that I am still moving despite the pain and difficulty.

The trouble with many of us is that we only focus on what we do not have, and forget all that we have been blessed with. This attitude makes for ingratitude.

Why should I be grateful? Most of the world's scriptures and nearly all the world's great spiritual masters emphasize that gratitude is essential for life to be beautiful. Most ordinary people too, would agree that complaining and criticizing can make life bitter and sour; and bitterness and sourness, as we know, are not anybody's flavours-of-the-week! Being grateful makes us positive, happy and optimistic; it helps us see the bright side of life. It teaches us the art of appreciation, which, I am afraid, is becoming a lost art for some of us today.

Some experts believe that we lack in the spirit of gratitude because we take things for granted. The street urchin into whose hands you drop a packet of biscuits looks up at you with gratitude and smiles happily. He has known what it is to be hungry, to go without food often times. He knows the value of those biscuits, which may not be dainty enough for our palates.

What do we do? Someone takes the trouble to shop and plan and cook and clean, so that a plate of hot food is put before us at regular intervals. We make faces and complain that the dish is too spicy or not spicy enough; that it is boring; that it is not our favourite recipe that has been served; and that the vegetables on the plate are not the ones we like!

Maybe, we need to go without the things we take for granted, to be able to appreciate what we have.

Gratitude is the foundation of a peaceful life, a secure and stable mind; it is also the essence of spirituality.

Acceptance in the spirit of gratitude unlocks the fullness in our lives. It can turn despair into faith, strife into harmony, chaos into order, and confusion into clear understanding. It restores peace into our hearts and helps us to look forward to the morrow in the faith that God is always with us.

It is not enough to speak of gratitude or enact deeds of gratitude – we must *live* gratitude by practicing acceptance of God's will in all conditions, in all incidents and accidents of life.

Let me tell you a beautiful story from the New Testament. Jesus was travelling to Jerusalem, when he saw a group of ten lepers standing at a distance from the road. In those days, lepers were forced to live in remote corners, out of sight of people. The prejudice and superstition about leprosy was so intense that people did not even want to see lepers. They always had to keep their distance. But as they saw Jesus approaching, they cried out to him in unison, 'Master, we beg you to heal us.'

Jesus looked at them with infinite compassion. Nine of them were Jews, while one was a Samaritan. Now, a Samaritan was regarded as an outcast in those days; but the common bond of suffering had obviously united these men. All of them appealed to him in unison, 'Master, heal us.'

Jesus said to them, 'Go to the priest,' and walked on.

The men were puzzled. 'We asked him for healing,' they said. 'Why does he ask us to go to a priest? What can the priest do for us?' However, they decided to follow the Master's instructions, and made their way to the temple.

On the way, a miracle happened. They began to feel better, they began to feel stronger. Their leprous sores began to disappear, and their skin became smooth, their faces turned bright. In the joy of being healed, they said, 'Let us run home to our families and share the good news with them.'

And so the nine Jews were off in a trice to return to their families. But the Samaritan went back to find Jesus. He walked all the way to catch up with the Master, and fell at his feet with tear-filled eyes, saying, 'Master, I do not have the words to express my gratitude to you. You have healed me! Thank you! Thank you! Thank you!

Jesus blessed the Samaritan and said to him, 'Ten were cleansed, only one has come. Where are the other nine?'

Moral of the story: even God misses something when you don't express gratitude to him for what He does for you. 'Thank you, God!' These words should always be on your lips, all the time.

When things are not going as we wish, we tend to develop 'tunnel vision', that is, we focus on the dark, negative side of life. However, we will do well to remember that it is always darkest before dawn and trial and adversity can be powerful agents of change that help us grow, evolve to become better human beings, and eventually make a success of our lives.

There are several things in our lives about which we choose not to be happy. Our 'wish list' for something different, something more, something other than what we possess extends to several aspects of our daily life.

Many affluent teenagers now carry cell phones, something which was unheard of even ten years ago. But not all of them are happy with these gadgets. Every six months or so, they wish to change models; they want more 'features'; they want the latest. When they are denied what they want, they sulk, and grumble, they wish they had richer and kinder parents.

Homemakers, mothers and wives wish to have better equipped kitchens. They want more gadgets, equipments, and aids to make their life easy. They want better furniture, more expensive curtains, and nicer clothes to wear. Men want better jobs, bosses, bigger cars, more money and more leisure time.

There's nothing wrong in wishing for any of these things. The problem arises when we develop a feeling of active discontent with what we are and what we have. Discontent leads to depression, and depression destroys our peace of mind.

A psychiatrist has described depression as 'anger turned inward.' We are angry with so many things and so many people; we are discontented with the way we live our lives, and we are angry at ourselves.

It was St Francis who prayed, 'Lord, give me the strength to change the things I can change, the patience to accept the things I cannot change, and the wisdom to know the difference.'

Wisdom is in accepting what you cannot change; what cannot be cured must be endured. This is not passive resignation or pessimistic self-denial. It is the way of wisdom which leads to peace.

We need to grow in the spirit of acceptance, for life is full of unexpected events. A dear one is snatched away from us suddenly. Initially, we are devastated; we weep, we shed bitter tears; we refuse to eat; we cannot sleep.

Wisdom is in accepting God's will, not with despair or resignation, but in peace, acceptance and faith, knowing that our journey through life has been perfectly planned by infinite love and infinite wisdom. There can be no mistake in God's plan for us.

Again and again, we try to run away from difficult situations; again and again, we rebel, react with anger and bitterness. How can we ever be at peace?

I remember that many years ago, an inspector of schools visited our Mira School in Pune. During an interaction with the students, he asked them, 'Tell me, where Pune is situated?' Many hands shot up, and the children gave the answer in chorus, 'In the state of Maharashtra.'

'Where is Maharashtra?' the inspector persisted.

'In India,' said the children.

'And where is India?'

'In Asia.'

'Can you tell me where is Asia?'

'In the world.'

'And where is the world?'

A pregnant silence prevailed. But one little girl came out with a sterling answer. 'Sir, the world is safe in the hands of God.'

The world is safe in the hands of God. Why then should we fret and fume over little disappointments and minor setbacks?

I must say that some of the people who suffer from pain and illness, some of the patients I have met in hospitals, are wonderful examples for all of us to emulate. They discover a lot to be grateful for in the midst of their pain and affliction; they enjoy what little respite they get from pain; they discover that such or such movements of their limbs can be accomplished without strain, and are ecstatic about it. They are happy to have visitors; they are grateful to the nursing staff; they thank their doctors for the relief they feel.

When you have made a choice, and the results are not what you expected them to be, choose to accept the consequences with gratitude.

God has a unique way of answering our prayers. Sometimes, He says, 'Yes'; sometimes, He says, 'No'; sometimes, He says, 'Wait'; sometimes, He says, 'Here is something better!' When He says, 'Yes', we are very happy. But all His answers are equally good for us: 'Yes', 'No', 'Wait', and 'Here is something better.'

One way to ensure that we always benefit from our prayers is to tell Him: 'God, grant me this wish, if it is for my good.' If a child cries for a knife and desperately wants to have it the mother will certainly not hand the knife over to him! Similarly, God, who is our father and mother, will give us only what is good for us.

If we ask Him for a flower, He may give us a seed or a sapling instead. It is for us to plant the seed, grow it and help it to blossom. This way, we learn to cherish and value His gifts.

Let us not despair, if our wishes are not granted. Our wishes will definitely be granted in a different form and at a different time. When we seek help from God, remember, we will always be in profit and never suffer a loss. Hence, let us not give up the attitude of gratitude.

Positive thinking, like gratitude, is not instantaneous. To be positive, to cultivate the spirit of thanksgiving, you have to put some effort. I am often told by a few friends, that in spite of much effort, some of them are unable to get rid of grudges, complaints and negativity. Maybe in some rare cases, one life is not sufficient to take away the negativism of numerous previous births. But you must continue your efforts, and some day, out of the blue, you will see the clouds disperse and the sun shining brightly!

How may we cultivate the attitude of gratitude in our daily life? Let me pass on to you a few practical suggestions:

1. Each day, when you awake, wash your face, brush your teeth, and stand in front of an open window and take at least three deep breaths, and thank God for the wonderful mechanism that is your body. Thank the Lord for the smooth functioning of your brain, for your precious eyesight, for the miraculous human faculties that God has blessed you with.
2. Always count your blessings! Conditions may be adverse. Dark clouds may appear on your horizon. Difficulties may threaten you. But make sure you always find something for which you feel grateful to God.
3. Appreciate others. Appreciate every little thing others do for you. Tell your spouse, 'Honey, where would I be without you?' Watch the wonderful effect these words will have on your relationship.
4. Never miss your daily appointment with God. Thank God for all His mercy to you during the last twenty-four hours. Actually, go over each of these blessings, and thank God for every one of them. Don't take it for granted because God knows everything anyway. It makes a difference when you actually recount them, and thank Him for it all.

5. Trust in the goodness and in the caring power of God. It was George Muller who said, 'The beginning of faith is the end of all worry and anxiety. And the beginning of worry and anxiety is the end of all faith.' In other words: 'Enter faith, exit worry!'

   Sadhu Vaswani said to us again and again, 'God upsets our plans to set up His own; and his plans are perfect.' He also said: 'Every disappointment is His appointment.' Trust in his goodness and caring power. Remember, God is too loving to punish, too wise to make a mistake. Therefore, everything that happens to us, there is a meaning of His mercy.
6. Let the words 'Thank you, God!' be on your lips all the time. When these words come from the depth of your heart, they will build for you a ladder of heightened consciousness, which you can climb to reach the very pinnacle of joy and peace, health and harmony! Keep on thanking God!
7. Thank God when the going is tough. Thank God even for difficult days and hard times. It is very easy to thank God when everything is going smoothly. But when things go wrong, we begin to lose faith in God; we disbelieve His wisdom; we even doubt His existence. When bitter experiences come to us, they come with a definite purpose. They are meant to make you better in some way or the other. Therefore, thank God even for adverse circumstances!
8. Let go, let go, let God! Let go of your problems. Life may be full of problems, but remember, in God there is a solution to every problem. Let God take over! Live like a child!

Surrender yourself to the Lord in this childlike trust, and you will find miracles daily happening in your life!

My Master, Sadhu Vaswani constantly praised God. We asked him, 'When difficulties come, what do you do?' He said, 'I praise the Lord.' We asked him, 'When your body is afflicted by illness and pain, what do you do?' He said, 'I still praise the Lord.' 'And when you are passing through a storm of life?' 'I still praise the Lord!'

That was the secret of Sadhu Vaswani's beautiful life! Let us take a leaf from the book of this holy man of God, this saint of compassion; let us praise God all the time! Let us always bear on our lips and in our hearts the beautiful words that constitute the Therapy of Thanksgiving: *Shukur! Shukur! Shukur!* Thank you, God! Thank you, God! Thank you, God!

Exercise

1. *What are the things in your life you are most grateful for?*
2. *How many of those things do you take for granted?*
3. *Write a note or better still, call up your close friends and family members to express your appreciation and gratitude to them for always being there for you.*
4. *Thank God for the great gift of life.*
5. *Choose the attitude of gratitude!*

POSITIVE AFFIRMATION SIX

I SHALL PRACTICE THE VIRTUE OF FORGIVENESS THAT HEALS ME AND OTHERS

One of the toughest choices we face in life, day after day, is the choice between resentment and forgiveness, strife and peace, discord and reconciliation.

Think of this commonplace situation: you are about to pick up speed and cross the green signal at a road junction, and the vehicle just ahead of you slows down, stalls, and comes to a standstill. In a few seconds, angry horns begin to blare and choice abuses are hurled at the hapless driver.

You have been given an appointment at a government office to collect an important certificate. You take the morning off to get to the office well before time, only to be told that the officer in charge has taken the day off.

You are scheduled to throw a party for a few friends at home and the preparations are on full swing in your kitchen. Out of the blue, your maid calls you up to say she can't come that day as she is unwell.

It is over a week since you instructed your subordinate to get a report ready for submission to the authorities. You ask for the report and you are told that he is still working on it.

And there are tougher situations that we cannot easily get over. A good friend criticizes you harshly in public, just because you have made a careless mistake. Your sister accuses you of being selfish because you have not been able to visit her ailing mother-in-law.

If you have been in one of these situations you will know that they are potentially 'explosive'!

Mind you, we have only touched banal, everyday disasters. Think of the more serious offences you have faced: most of us still harbour bitterness and grudges against those who insulted us, betrayed our trust or cheated us. Like cancer, the anger and hurt are festering within our hearts.

When you think of some of those conflicts many of us might not have faced, like coping with adultery, sexual abuse, or domestic violence, can you imagine the anger, the grief and the rage the victims must be holding against their perpetrators?

But to every one of you who have faced provocations, major or minor, for each one who has had to bear the brunt of betrayal and offence, let me say: you too have a choice. You may choose an unforgiving attitude and the cancer of resentment and bitterness; or you may choose to forgive, forget, heal yourself and feel the freedom of compassionate leniency!

I can well understand the hurt and pain and the deep sense of betrayal people feel, when they have been victims of the evil, wrong and sinful choices other people have made: I can well imagine them crying out in anguish against any appeal for forgiveness, let alone reconciliation, 'How can you speak to me of forgiveness? If only you knew the pain that I have been put through in my life, you would never expect me to forgive the people who inflicted such suffering on me.'

There are grown men who regard themselves as failures because their fathers told them repeatedly that they would be no good in life.

There are women suffering from incurable low self-esteem because a teacher called them stupid or foolish.

There are young ladies who endure severe eating disorders because they were bullied by friends for being overweight.

Forgiveness is not always easy. How can parents forgive the murderer of their children? How can mothers forgive the rapists of their daughters? How can anyone forgive those who have massacred their family and friends?

I am the first to admit it is not easy. But the alternative is to become like those offenders: intransigent, cruel and unfeeling. Forgiveness releases you from the fetters of hatred, and frees you from the pain, shame and humiliation of the past, which is thankfully, dead and gone.

Think of the people who have endured rape, abuse, violence and psychological torture. Is it right to tell them, 'Forgive and forget! Let go, let God!'

Yes! The perpetrators of evil will have to face their karmic consequences in ways and means that we may never know. But the victims, the injured innocent ones must heal themselves, make themselves whole and carry on with their lives.

And no, I am not being arbitrary or insensitive or uncaring. I don't want you to live with the terrible woes and the festering wounds of your past! You need to be free from pain and hurt and lifelong suffering; therefore, I beseech you earnestly, choose the way of compassion, forgiveness and healing. You owe it to yourself. The person who wronged you committed the offence in the past. Will you continue to relive the sufferings for a lifetime? Will you continue to wrong yourself, redoubling the hurt and pain?

Are there no limits to forgiveness? Would forgiveness not mean exonerating, excusing, or condoning evil actions? Would this not be immoral, not to speak of it being unethical and unjust?

Writer and poet, C. S. Lewis, argued that forgiveness transcends the idea of human fairness: it sometimes involves pardoning those things that can't be pardoned at all. It is much more than excusing. When we excuse someone, we simply brush their mistakes aside. As he puts it, 'If one was not really to blame, then there is nothing to forgive. In that sense forgiveness and excusing are almost opposites.' He concludes, 'Real forgiveness means looking steadily at the sin, the sin that is left over without any excuse, after all allowances have been made, and seeing it in all its horror, dirt, meanness and malice, and nevertheless being wholly reconciled to the person who has done it. That, and only that is forgiveness.'

May I add, forgiveness is also above justice. Justice seeks to punish; forgiveness seeks reconciliation. As Shakespeare puts it so beautifully in his play, *The Merchant of Venice*,

> Though justice be thy plea, consider this:
> That in the course of justice none of us should see salvation.
> We do pray for mercy
> And that same prayer doth teach us all to render
> The deeds of mercy.

Choose to forgive and forget! It is the best choice you can make.

It is not for nothing that Jesus gave us the beautiful prayer, which says: 'Forgive us our trespasses, as we forgive those who trespass against us.' And no, Jesus is not teaching us to ask for a quid pro quo: He is not telling His Father, if you forgive my sins, I shall forgive those who sinned against me. It is God who must forgive all of us our trespasses, big and small. And He is far more gracious, compassionate, loving and forgiving than we can ever hope to be! What the Lord's Prayer teaches us is that we cannot freely embrace God's love and compassion for us if we are not willing to forgive our fellow human beings.

The inner channels within us, through which God's love and forgiveness can flow into our hearts, cannot and must not clogged by hardened bitterness and grudges. In other words, our incapacity and unwillingness to forgive and forget those who have hurt us must not become an insurmountable block in the way of our receiving God's grace and blessings!

Choose to forgive and forget! Choose to move on into the future leaving the woes and burdens of the past behind you. How long will you carry those exhausting, emaciating loads of anger and misery?

Forgiveness can transform your life and open the floodgates of well-being, abundance, and joy into your world.

We all take forgiveness as a birthright when it comes to ourselves: 'But I didn't mean it,' we say. 'That was not what I intended.' When it comes to others, we are always miserly about it.

If I choose not to forgive someone, I carry a grudge within myself. This grudge disturbs my peace of mind, my richest treasure. I refuse to forgive someone for what he has done to me. I may not show it, the other person may not know it, but the bitterness festers like an untreated infectious wound in my heart. I carry the cross! Not to forgive another is a punishment that I inflict upon myself. It is like locking myself in a narrow cell and throwing away the key.

To cling to resentments is to harm oneself, to walk the way of spiritual death. To choose to let go of resentments is to walk the way that leads to a life of freedom and fulfilment. The person who holds on to anger or resentment is, without his knowledge, causing damage to himself from within. The person who forgives enters a new life of gentle peacefulness. Forgiveness is its own reward. It is the forgiver rather than the forgiven who receives the greater benefit. Therefore, we must choose forgiveness rather than anger or revenge!

The spirit of forgiveness is lacking in our lives today. And therefore, our stress keeps increasing. It keeps on mounting, until it breaks out in the form of some physical ailment or the other.

A learned professor of great academic repute was engaging his class at the university. Having delivered an introduction, he pointed to one of the students and asked him to read aloud from the text.

The student arose and began to read, holding his book in his left hand. 'That's not the way to behave in class,' said the professor sharply. 'Take your book in your right hand and be seated.'

The student stopped short. After a moment or two, he silently held up his right arm; he did not have a right hand!

The class grew strangely silent. Everyone felt uncomfortable and pained.

The professor sat still, dumbfounded; then he rose from his seat and walked slowly down to where the young man stood. He put his arm around him and said with tears in his eyes, 'I am truly sorry. I have spoken in haste. Will you please forgive me?'

Forgiveness is the precious lubricant, which keeps all our relationships smooth and friction-free. We often find doors and windows and gates beginning to groan and squeak when they have not been oiled. So do we begin to squeak under stress; forgiveness can take the squeaks away.

A young mother brought her two quarrelling children together and insisted that they made up with each other. 'Say sorry to your brother,' she said to her daughter. 'And you; say sorry to your sister!'

'Sorry!' snapped the girl. 'I am saying sorry from the outside because mummy asked me to. But inside I am still very angry with you!'

This is not the spirit of true forgiveness. It does not lie in words or phrases. It must come from the heart within.

Why should we forgive?

A distinguished psychologist lists the following points as the practical benefits of forgiveness:

- First, it stimulates our spiritual growth, which is stunted, stopped in its tracks by an unforgiving nature. Forgiveness releases us from the deadening burden of resentment and blame and allows us to use our spiritual energy in constructive ways.
- Second, the act of forgiveness restores our vitality, stamina and zest for life.
- Third, it restores peace and harmony in our lives.
- Fourth, it allows us to live a more abundant life, with an uncluttered soul, an unburdened heart and a mind free from resentment and recriminations.

Resentment and anger are destructive emotions. They damage us from within. And the damage is manifested in symptoms that are almost unbearable: the inability to go to sleep in peace; a gnawing feeling in the pit of the stomach; a heavy burden of sorrow on the heart; a throbbing headache; a blinding pain.

No wonder Emerson wrote, 'For every minute you remain angry, you give up sixty seconds of peace of mind.'

Forgiveness holds the promise of freedom and relief from such suffering.

Before I close, let me narrate to you a story which will make you wonder: Is such forgiveness possible?

The Amish community are a group of Christian church fellowships that form a sub-group of the Mennonite churches. The Amish are known for simple living, plain dressing, and the reluctance to adopt many conveniences of modern technology. Not many people have heard of them. But their practices and beliefs came into the limelight worldwide due to a tragic incident that happened ten years ago. Let me give you the story as it was reported in newspapers and TVs on that dark day.

On Monday morning, 2 October 2006, twenty-five Amish children were settling into their class routine at a one-room Amish school in Nickel Mines, Pennsylvania. All of a sudden, a gunman entered the class and ordered the teacher and all the boys to leave the school at once. He was Charles Roberts, a thirty-two-year-old father of four, who had become mentally unstable following the death of his baby daughter.

Despite her repeated pleas and protests, the teacher was thrown out of the class; the boys followed her, trembling with fear. Roberts then proceeded to tie up the feet of the ten remaining girls, so that they could not move or attempt to escape. Then, in a horrible execution ceremony, he prepared to shoot the children with an automatic rifle and four hundred rounds of ammunition that he had specially brought for the task. The oldest hostage, a thirteen-year-old girl, begged Roberts, 'Shoot me first and let the little ones go.' Refusing her offer, he opened fire on all of them, killing five of them instantly and leaving the others critically wounded.

The police, who had by then been alerted, stormed the building. Roberts shot himself before he could be captured.

His motivation? 'I'm angry at God for taking my little daughter,' he told the little girls before the massacre.

The story captured the attention of broadcast and print media in the United States and around the world. By Tuesday morning, some fifty television crews had crowded into the small village of Nickel Mines, staying on for five days with their broadcast vans and technical equipment, until the killer and the killed were buried.

The blood was barely dry on the schoolhouse floor when Amish parents brought words of forgiveness to the family of the man who had slain their children. Their hearts still heavy and their eyes still wet with tears of grief, their memories still fresh of the funerals where they had buried their own children, grieving Amish families accounted for half of the seventy-five people who attended the killer's burial. Roberts' widow was deeply moved by their presence, as Amish families greeted her and her three children. The forgiveness went beyond talk and grave-side presence: the Amish also supported a fund for the shooter's family.

Loud television presenters and incredulous viewers wondered how it was possible that such forgiveness could be offered so spontaneously for such a heinous crime. On chat shows and live panel discussions, the topic was not guns or violence, but the power of forgiveness. Seasoned media watchers agreed that forgiveness had, in fact, eclipsed the tragic story, trumping the violence and arresting the world's attention.

Within a week of the murders, Amish forgiveness was the talking point in more than 2,400 news stories; from *Washington Post* to *Khaleej Times*, from Larry King to Oprah, hundreds of media outlets hailed the spirit of the forgiving Amish. Three weeks after the shooting, 'Amish forgiveness' had appeared in 2,900 news stories worldwide and on 534,000 websites.

This story has valuable lessons for all of us. How could the Amish do this? What did this act mean to them? And how might their witness prove useful to the rest of us?

Exercise

1. *Do you need to forgive yourself? Compassion, like charity, must begin at home. If you are angry with yourself about something, let it go!*
2. *Make a list of all the people who caused you the most hurt. Call out their names aloud, one by one and forgive them. Actually say, 'Mr X, I forgive you.' 'Ms Y, I forgive you.' Bless*

them and release them, and feel the tremendous sense of release that this brings to you.

3. *Are you one of those people who allow anger and resentment to build up over little things? Practice the art of letting go.*
4. *Choose to forgive and forget!*

POSITIVE AFFIRMATION SEVEN

I SHALL CHOOSE KINDNESS

Choose to react to the world with kindness, courtesy and love; believe me – they will come back to you manifold.

The Dalai Lama tells us, 'Be kind whenever possible.' He adds, 'It is always possible.'

Kindness and courtesy are like the proverbial bread you cast upon the waters. 'After many days,' the Bible tells us, 'you will find it again.'

Note, we are not being told to look left and right, consider pros and cons carefully, judge where our kindness is directed, make sure that those who are at the receiving end are worthy of our generosity, or anything like that. 'Cast thy bread upon the waters.' Show kindness without any strings attached; don't look at what's in it for you.

'When you have a choice to be right, or to be kind, choose to be kind,' said Wayne Dyer, the psychologist who turned to spirituality, and made the power of both these disciplines accessible to his many readers. Choose kindness and love! I think this is the reason why grandparents, especially grandmothers, are such great favourites with the children!

Who among us can put up with rudeness, discourtesy and bad temper? All of us like to be treated with politeness, understanding and patience. To be at the receiving end of such treatment, we must first learn to treat others with kindness and respect.

The children's novel *Wonder* was published in 2012. It became such a hit with everyone that it was made into a movie, and also inspired a nationwide anti-bullying campaign in the United States. The book is about a young boy with a facial deformity, and the treatment he faces when, after an initial period of home-schooling, his parents decide to put him in a school where he can grow up with other children of his age. The boy, Auggie, meets with great kindness and understanding from the Head of the school, his class teacher and a few friends; but there is a group of boys who bully him mercilessly and even a few parents who feel he ought not to be in the school with other children. Dealing with just one year of school, the book lays bare the cruelty and harshness that children face from school bullies.

Auggie survives the ordeal and comes out with flying colours, by learning to accept the kindness of friends and forgiving the rudeness of the bullies. At the year-end graduation ceremony, Auggie is awarded the 'Henry Ward Beecher Medal,' which 'honours students who have been notable or exemplary in certain areas throughout the school year'. The head, Mr Tushman, tells the assembled students, 'If every single person in this room made it a rule that wherever you are, whenever you can, you will try to act a little kinder than is necessary, the world would be a better place.'

Are you teaching your children to be kind, courteous and compassionate? The best way to do this is by being their role model, setting a personal example which they can follow!

I happen to know many people who have been treated harshly at work for failures and mishaps for which they were not personally responsible. Some superior officers just need to unleash their bad temper on someone – anyone – and these poor employees become the scapegoats, bearing the brunt of their wrath. Is there a delay in the delivery of supplies? Is there a miscommunication from a client? Is there a delay from the bank? The temper tantrums, abuse, name-calling and finger-pointing are all directed at the hapless subordinate who happens to be present, although everyone knows it is not his fault.

People with such a volatile nature and highly explosive temperaments create a work environment of high stress and fear. Their lack of kindness and common courtesy in stressful situations scar the psyche of the employees and no amount of sweet talking and increments and parties after the event can make up for what the employees go through when they are facing the brunt of the boss' bad temper.

Even in such situations – even in business environments where millions of dollars are at stake – one can tackle the situation with courtesy and politeness.

If there was one business magnate who earned the title of 'benign boss' it was India's own J. R. D. Tata. He set out to analyze why workers felt hostile and mistrustful of the management, and realized that they felt that they were just like cogs in a soulless machine. He set out to make them feel they were valued members of a friendly and humane organization. Tata Steel was the first to have a dedicated full-fledged HR department from early days. The company pioneered the eight-hour day in 1912, long before the principle had been accepted in the United States or Europe (Britain introduced the twelve-hour day in 1911). They also introduced leave-with-pay in 1920, while in India, this was established by law only in 1945. Tata Steel set up a provident fund in 1920, which was not legalized until 1952.

You may call this a smart or a progressive business practice. But all this was pioneered by a man and a company who knew the value of philanthropy and kindness! 'To be a leader,' J. R. D. Tata said, 'you have got to lead human beings with affection.'

But what if you face rudeness and unkindness in any given situation?

Don't choose the obvious reaction: a tit for tat retaliation. It is so easy to respond to rudeness with greater rudeness; it is so easy to join the blame-and-scream game. Diffuse the strained situation with calm, loving kindness. Or, to borrow the vocabulary of Eric Berne, gently lead the tantrum-kicking child away and invite the sane and sensible adult to take over the situation.

Psychologists say that it is very often people who desperately need to be loved who act in a very unloving, unkind manner. How do we deal with such people? Once again, the Bible shows us the way. 'Love is patient, love is kind. It does not envy, it does not boast, it is not proud.' (1 Corinthians, 13:4)

It takes enormous courage to treat a yelling, abusive, rude person with patience and understanding. This does not mean we are allowing them to get away with abuse and verbal violence. But the chances are they may be shamed into following your lead.

Let us face it: this abusive, unkind, rude person may be your superior at work, your spouse, your irate offspring or even your best friend. You can't just let them walk out of your life. The alternative is to treat them with respect and loving kindness and put yourself in their shoes to understand their feelings.

Jessica Walsh and Timothy Goodman were two self-centred look-ahead professionals, who often failed to notice what was going on around them, so busy were they with their work and social life. Suddenly, they began to ask themselves some tough questions:

So, why is it so difficult to be kind at times? How can we become less judgmental of others and ourselves? We tend to only see what we want to see, hear what we want to hear, and surround ourselves with people who share our own experiences and tastes. Countless scientific studies, newspaper articles, religious texts, and self-help books have tried to help us become kinder people, but how often do we really put that advice into practice?

Like the rest of us, Tim and Jessie had also heard sayings like, 'Treat others the way you would like to be treated' and 'Don't judge another until you've walked a mile in their shoes'. Tim and Jessie decided, one fine day, to take these sentiments and literally apply them to their own lives. They created a 12-step programme designed to change behaviours, (you could also call it a 12-step experiment) to confront their own apathy and selfishness.

May I share with you the programme they designed? (The titles may startle you at first: Tim and Jessie are creative people.)

1. *Can I Help You?* This was the question they asked of perfect strangers in difficult situations.
2. *Open Your Eyes.* They put up missing people signs and posters all over New York and realized very few people bothered to look. (I don't know if this is a good or bad thing, but people took more note of missing dogs than they did of missing people!)
3. *Switch it Up!* They chose people working in jobs which we always try to ignore and regard as a nuisance: random sales-people, interviewers, people selling products that no one wants to buy, and the like. They tried to be kinder to such people conscientiously.
4. *Don't Beat Yourself Up!* They tried to be kinder to themselves as they relived situations in which they had behaved badly. They learned to forgive themselves.

5. *Forgive and Forget.* They faced people who had hurt them in the past and learnt to let go of the bitterness and resentment.
6. *Face Yourself.* They learnt to come to terms with their own fears and insecurities and face their weaknesses without letting this affect their behaviour towards others.
7. *Kill Them with Kindness.* They picked people who had been unkind, ungenerous to them in the past, and tried to understand them better by being nice to them and doing something kind for them.
8. *Walk a Mile in their Shoes.* This was designed to understand and empathize with people who chose to be different from the rest; to understand their very different lifestyles and what motivated them, instead of simply dismissing them as freaks or weirdos.
9. *Go Big or Go Home.* This was specially meant for the people they were closest to, and neglected sadly for the same reason! They went out of their way to show their appreciation and gratitude to the people they took for granted.
10. *Pay it Forward!* In this innovative experiment, they left little wallets with money all over New York's sidewalks with notes to the strangers who picked them up, asking them to spend the money on acts of kindness. Tim and Jessie also performed random acts of kindness to strangers.
11. *Wear a Smile.* They walked around New York City and smiled at everyone; everyone they came across. They wondered how many people would smile back at them!

12. *Dive Deep.* They decided to start a website and a blog to share their experiences with others and invite others to join their experiment.

For twelve months, Tim and Jessie attempted to open their hearts, eyes and minds to become kinder, more empathetic people. And for both of them, it was a worthwhile learning experience.

The divinity in a person is seen in his/her actions of kindness, forgiveness, love, and compassion. The demonic element expresses itself in actions of revenge, envy, jealousy, the burning fire of anger, cruelty and harsh criticism of others.

There was a time, when our families exuded the warmth of love and serenity of peace. The family members overlooked each other's faults, gave each other understanding, love and tolerance; they forgave each other's mistakes, supported one another in times of crisis, sustained each other in times of grief and tragedy. The families bonded in harmony, vibrating calmness and happiness. There was loving kindness in the elders. Whenever the youngsters went wayward or wrong, the elders tenderly enfolded them in love and kindness, and brought them on to the right track.

This is one of the strongest reasons to keep the three-generation joint-family alive!

Loving kindness does not require a hefty wallet, strong limbs, heroic deeds, or great and austere sacrifices. A helping hand, a friendly word or gesture, a kind smile will more than suffice! And let me add, in the words of Mark Twain:

'Kindness is a language which the deaf can hear and the blind can read!'

Kindness binds the world together in the bond of unity and peace. I will conclude with a quote from the book *Sorrow Mountain: The Journey of a Tibetan Warrior Nun*, 'Remember the words of Buddha: "In separateness lies the world's greatest misery, in compassion lies the world's true strength"'.

Exercise

1. *Are you always kind to yourself and to those loved ones who are closest to you?*
2. *Do you perform random acts of kindness for strangers and people you meet?*
3. *Do you always wait for others to smile at you / wish you before you reciprocate?*
4. *Have you ever paused to take stock of God's kindness to you?*
5. *Choose kindness as a way of life!*